COPENHAVER COUNTRY

By Howard Copenhaver

Author of "They Left Their Tracks"
and
"More Tracks"

COPENHAVER COUNTRY

By Howard Copenhaver

Author of "They Left Their Tracks"
and
"More Tracks"

ILLUSTRATIONS BY LESLIE-DRAKE ROBINSON
Copyright By The Artist, 1996

Copyright 1996 by Howard Copenhaver

Published in the United States of America

ISBN 0-912299-75-7 (Hardcover)
ISBN 0-912299-66-5 (Softcover)

STONEYDALE PRESS PUBLISHING COMPANY
523 Main Street • P.O. Box 188
Stevensville, Montana 59870
Phone: 406-777-2729

TABLE OF CONTENTS

DEDICATION

Well, here we go again. I dedicate this book to all of my friends all over the great U.S. who have followed my "Tracks." Also to those young ones who are just starting to make a trail that they can look back through great memories and remember their own "Tracks."

Gook luck reading. If you don't like it, just put it in the oval office and trip the lever that flushes all down the drain.

Howard

FOREWORD

*Ever since Howard Copenhaver's first book, "**They Left Their Tracks,**" came out in 1990 and we traveled with him from one book-signing event to another, it has been obvious that he'd captured in that wonderful book, which incidentally is now in its seventh printing, a rare and deeply moving, even magical, insight into what wilderness means to both those who live in and near it, and those who come to visit it once in awhile.*

But it has also been obvious over that same period that numerous other stories, some humorous, some sad, some simply uplifting, were still inside Howard. And many were, are, marvelous stories! But they came out only fragmentally, lifting from his subconscious mind to the surface only when some person or event jogged his memory with sufficient force to bring those wonderful memories into his conscious mind. When that occurred, he'd share some of those stories, or portions of them, with those who came to his book signings, and the inevitable piece of advice would ensue: "Howard, you ought to write another book."

Now those of us who have known Howard for many, many years and who have listened spell-bound to his tales of the wilderness and grizzly bears and the elk hunters, and his beloved horses and mules, have felt the same way. Sometimes we've even wanted to scream, "Howard, let a few more of those stories out! Get them down on paper!"

*And therein was the rub. Those memory jogs at the various book signings were part of a natural process wherein a storyteller whose past tradition had been oral is at his natural best. And for those of us who worked with Howard to convert his story-telling method from oral to written in "**They Left Their Tracks,**" it was very clear just how difficult, even strenuous, the transition from one tradition to the other was for Howard. Writing was, for him as it is to most people who try it seriously, an incredibly laborious* *process. Writing seldom comes easy for anyone, not good writing, anyway, and for someone from the oral story-telling tradition it is even more arduous because it not only takes longer but it requires the use of a different, more demanding internal voice. Words on paper have no force behind them but themselves! And how they're put together!*

Howard experienced this first-hand, often with overwhelming frustration. Those memory jogs that took place at a book signing, or during a visit with a friend or acquaintance, coincidentally freed Howard up to respond, spontaneously — to tell those stories orally. That's natural. It was this tradition, refined over the years around hundreds, even thousands, of campfires in the Bob Marshall Wilderness and elsewhere, that spawned his own adventure in story-telling. And he'd fall into the oral story-telling process almost without thinking. But, fired up by these memories brought once more to the light, Howard would get going on his "new book," and then, a few days later when the stories somehow just wouldn't convert to the written page, he'd call and express his frustration. And disappointment that he was having such a hard time of it.

*Of course he found the muse for a time, when still in the shadow of the release of "**They Left Their Tracks,**" and the magic returned. He shared a few of those stories that came back during that period in his excellent second book, "**More Tracks,**" but even so he knew there was, within him, some more stories and episodes from his long life in the wilderness, and the semi-wild country around Ovando, that wanted to be told. For a couple of years he struggled with those dimly-lit memories to bring them to the surface once again, and to write them out with the same fervor he, and we, knew were in them when he was simply "telling stories."*

Then he lit on the notion that he should have someone tape record his oral story-telling sessions. But that didn't work, either. He found that he was playing to the recorder and the magic wasn't there when he looked at the transcription. So he gave up on the idea of using the recordings as a memory jog and struggled on, for months, to put together, on paper, a series of stories that he felt measured up to what he wanted to accomplish with a new book, which he often said would probably be his last.

He called me one afternoon a little over a year ago and said he had some stories for me to look at — seven, to be exact. I told him to send them down and that we'd look them over. He did, and we did. And we sent them back up to Ovando with a note that they needed some work. And that not only did they need some polishing, but that there would have to be a bunch more of them. And, for a summer and a long, cold Montana winter, Howard continued to struggle not only with the idea of doing another book but actually getting at it, writing it.

And then one wonderful, sunny day this past February, Howard was on the phone. He was excited, even ecstatic. The ideas and the words were flowing once more. The drama of the wilderness and how it had always inspired him was back; I could hear it in his voice as he spoke! And, miracle of miracles, he'd once again found his voice as a writer! He'd tossed out those seven stories and started all over. And not only were the memories rising up from his subconscious mind (My term, not his. He said something about the 'old noggin working again') but they were coming up clear and powerful and emotive. The campfire was burning, once again!

How had this come to be? It seems that an old friend, one with whom he'd traveled a good number of miles many years ago on an elk hunt or two in the wilderness, had called him up to simply tell him how much he'd enjoyed reading Howard's first book, "They Left Their Tracks." And in the process, this friend made reference to how much he appreciating Howard "doing all this backtracking for his friends."

And that was the key. Howard realized at that moment why he hadn't been able to summon up his story-telling magic as he'd tackled the job of writing a new book. It had been because he was trying to reach deep inside himself and, literally, pull those memories into the present. He wasn't going back in his memories, backtracking if you will, to where he'd find detail and lost parts of the trail. And he immediately put himself back into the same mode of thinking, the same muse, if you will, that had enlivened his earlier books — going over old trails, following the tracks to where the action would be found. And, in his backtracking, the people and places and events of his stories once again came to life... Howard Copenhaver, the oral storyteller, was once again freed up to share portions of his life's trail with us, on paper.

The result, of course, is this book. And we originally thought of titling it "Backtracking," making the obvious play on the use of the word "tracks" from Howard's two previous books. But we knew the title should be a bit more suggestive than that, so we thought of using "Backtracking In Copenhaver Country," and that is still my favorite. But Howard pointed out that the stories in this book are really those of a man whose entire life, wherever he's been and whatever he's done, has been shaped by the land in which he's lived and worked, by family and friends and others. That land, that place, is, in his mind, "Copenhaver Country" and because of that, he felt that was what he was sharing within the pages of this book. He knows, and we know, that what he shares with you on the following pages is but a part of the legacy that comes from this grand land of ours. These are, simply, stories from "Copenhaver Country."

*It is a wonderful, witty, occasionally touching, invigorating legacy Howard shares within these pages — and we are delighted to make this book, **"Copenhaver Country,"** by our friend, master storyteller Howard Copenhaver, the first in what will become an ongoing series of books of a similar vein to be called the "Stoneydale Press Legacy Series." These books will feature titles of a special Montana flavor and, hopefully, will offer unique insights into this good land of ours. There's more to come, of course, but for now we're delighted that "Number One" in this series is presently in your hands. It contains stories written by Howard Copenhaver, and it's a dandy. Enjoy!*

Dale A. Burk
Stevensville, Montana
July 25, 1996

INTRODUCTION

Welcome to Copenhaver Country! You're in my country now, so set your hair down and be one of the family as we do some backtracking in my part of the world. There's coffee in the pot and cups nearby, fish in the creek and elk on those ridges right up next to the sky.

You know, as we sit here shooting the bull, there is only three things that are worthwhile: friends, country and memories. By country I mean right here where we sit, in my own Ovando country. Only God could have made this great Northwest. The people, the solitude of the mountains and the experiences, nature, wild game, and the people who have allowed me to be part of and to share with so many caring people.

If I were to write my own epitaph for a headstone, it would go something like this:

As you are
I once was
You'll follow me
So be prepared

But, you know, I'm afraid some crazy joker would come along with a can of red paint and print right below it:

To follow you
I'm not content
Until I'm sure
Which way you went!

You can't take any of these memories or experiences with you. So I've tried to write them down for someone else to enjoy and mebby laugh at when I'm gone. It's all history. It's past.

Two poems written by some of my long-time-ago outfitting guests sum it all up and tell it as it really is, the feelings gained by visitors in the summer and hunters in the fall, along with the opportunity of knowing yourself better than you did before.

How many times I've gone to sleep to the strains of "Oh Danaher" being sung by guests under star studded skies, I can't remember.

O DANAHER
(To be sung to the tune of Oh Tennenbaum)
Dedicated to the Helena Wilderness Riders

I'm ridin' to a land I know
Where game abounds and campfires glow.
It's in Montana's Wilderness
A place that blessed by God's caress.

CHORUS:
*   O Danaher — Oh Danaher*
Take me back to the Danaher
Where the deer and elk all run free
Where the pine and fir reach out to me.

Oh that's the place that I love best.
Oh Danaher — Montana wilderness.

The mountains bound a wide prairie green
Where native trout play in a stream.
The switchback trails lead to passes high
Where a man can hear the eagle's cry.

CHORUS:
We riders come distant lairs
To ride these trails and leave our cares
We toast his land on every score
May God keep it wild forevermore.

For those who can't live without solitude and natural beauty, "Oh, Danaher" sure spells wilderness in my book.

For the more hearty soul who likes the challenge and excitement and the feeling of satisfaction and success I give you the "Saga of the Bull."

SAGA OF THE BULL

This head on the wall is to prove to all
That he is a mighty spread.
He is the only game that is worth the name
So we saved his head.

The elk still stands in this western land
The greatest beast of all.
And, seek him out or do without,
That's the theme of the sportsman's call.

The Redman's cow is vanishing now
And so is the grizzly bear.
Now the bear, the moose, the Canadian goose,
They are all easy game when found,
But, come with me and you'll agree
We have covered a lot of ground.

Your shots may score ten or more,
But on elk that won't quite do.
He'll leave that place without a trace
Even though his heart is shot through.

So all of you boys with your pop-gun toys,
If it's a man you want to be,
Go get your gun and we'll have some fun.
When that elk calls, follow me.

Now heed not I of a wintry sky
Or an untracked forest hill,

For I will ride with any guide
Until I make my kill.

I want you to know and I'm telling you so,
He has a right to brag.
For he is a man that's proven he can
Conquer that mighty stag.

Now if you don't understand what I mean, mebby this story of Mary will help.

Many years ago I had a group of men and their wives on a sight-seeing trip. No hunting, no fishing, just riding, hiking, camping out-of-doors, enjoying the flora and fauna. The only shots taken were with a camera.

It was a leisurely trip with no long days in the saddle. We'd make camp early where the guests could spend two or three hours climbing a high peak or just strolling along a scenic stream soaking up nature, then back to camp for supper and an evening around a campfire singing and telling stories.

It was in the first part of August, beautiful weather with a full moon at night. The moon and stars seemed to brush the tops of the mountains. You had to wonder how they got past those peaks without tumbling rocks to the valley floor. Have you ever seen it that way? You can't describe it, you have to be there and see it.

This particular night we were camped in a big alpine basin on the head of Moose Creek, right up against the China Wall. There is a little lake up there and breathtaking views any way you look. We'd had a steak supper, followed by a campfire sing and story-telling session. Then, slowly couples would mosey off to their tepees for the night. We planned to arise early and get on the trail by 6:30 to view the mountain goat along the wall and elk in the big basins before we came to Larch Hill Pass. This trail leads you down the west side of the Continental Divide to White River and the big basin just under Silvertip Mountain, a great place to see goat, elk, and grizzly bear.

I was about to douse the fire with a bucket of water when here came Mary with a blanket wrapped around her. She said, "Howard, I'll put it out. I just want to sit here for awhile by myself."

I headed for my sack. Four o'clock comes early and quick, even up in the high country. When I arose the next morning to start a fire and make coffee, it was four o'clock in the morning and there sat Mary, all wrapped up in her blanket and the fire gone out.

I said, "Mary, what are you doing? Are you sick?"

"No," she said, "I just couldn't sleep last night."

I asked her if she was tired, or cold, or what. Mary responded, "At first it was so beautiful, with the moon and stars, but then it got so quiet it hurt my ears. I was afraid to move because I might break the silence and spoil it all."

Howard Copenhaver
Ovando, Montana
Early Summer, 1996

TRIXI'S

Now if you've read my other books, you've probably noticed that I always end up at Trixi's somehow.

Well now, I'm a nice guy but I don't mind using people if I can get by with it. First off, Leo and Verla are great people, have given me much support in my writing and honored me with a great party when my books came out. Thank you Leo and Verla.

And, when I have doubts about a story for a book, I take it up to Trixi's. I sit on a bar stool and Verla reads the story to herself. As nasty as I am, I watch her face and try to read her thoughts so I can tell if it's good or bad. Now, Verla will say, "Oh, this is great," but I throw some of them in the File 13 anyway. I know she's to nice to hurt my feelings. Thanks again.

About a year ago when I was looking for something to write about Verla in my book, I'd had no luck till the other day I was told about an incident and "bang," I had a story.

It seems it was along about 10:00 or 10:30 one evening last summer when we had the most terrible electric storm ever in the Ovando area — weird rain and lightning and thunder that deafened you. Now, Verla and Leo live in a house surrounded by tall pine and fir trees — and Verla is dreadfully scared of lightning.

Leo, more of a "so what" guy, was trying to console her in the midst of that terrible storm and he said, "Honey, if the lightning hits you, you'll never feel it anyway. If you hear the thunder, it's already missed you."

"Oh, but Honey, I'd feel so much safer up at the bar," she replied.

This went on for a time and, finally, Leo saw that he was not going to get any sleep with things the way they were, so he fired up the old pickup and said, "O.K. lets go to the bar."

Margaret and Howard Copenhaver flank the "celebration cake" specially made for them by Verla and Leo Bush (center) upon the release of Howard's first book, They Left Their Tracks, held at and sponsored by Trixi's in Ovando.

"Thank you, Honey, you're so thoughtful," she said, and they jumped into the pickup and headed for Trixi's.

The lightning flashes were so bright Leo couldn't see the road part of the time, and when they drove up to the parking lot in front of the bar, KER-BOOM, another crash of thunder sounded and a jagged streak came out of the black sky and hit that old Trixi's Bar right in the middle.

Out went all the lights and smoke puffed out of the roof. But no flames ensued.

Now, as I said before, Verla is a very attractive lady but it's unbelievable that she could attract lightning like she does. And the other day, I noticed, as she and Leo were heading off on a vacation, that Verla had an old-time lady's hat pin sticking out of her hair. I said to Leo, "Why does she have that hat pin in her hair and no hat?"

"Easy," he said. "That ain't a hat pin. It's a lightning rod!"

BICYCLES, BULLS AND RUSTY

I'm sure you've heard the old saying that "A farmer is the greatest gambler of all."

I'm not sure that's always right. Sure he fights time, weather, grasshoppers, insects, frost and broken down machinery. And also the banker's interest and old age. It takes a long time to make a million off a hunk of dirt that needs some kind of fertilizer and fewer rocks. But you take a rancher; he fights all of these, plus old Mother Nature and her governing of romance among young animals.

A rancher fights them all except the banker, 'cause he knows when these bulls and heifers are ready for sale the price will be down to where the banker will have it all anyway. So why not be a cowboy and have fun riding a horse, roping a calf and singin' a western song? Sure good music. Just ridin' down the canyon looking for someone else's girl. (Seldom find one there in the moonlight but there's that gamblin' chance so we have to take it.) When we were young and when we get old, might as well keep goin' because it's too late to quit.

Well this all happened to me and my brothers one time when we were working at ranching. We were raising blue ribbon bulls and heifers. Good ones, too. One Sunday afternoon, we were all taking it easy. Winter was over and cows are out on green grass. No hay to pitch — just pour the grain in the feeders for that bunch of (we hope!) prize bulls. They were all fenced in the bull lot and we'd just built that fence new, four wires on top of 24 inches of woven wire. Not a chance of a leak in it.

Even the saddle horses were in the little pasture down south of the house. Everybody was snoozin' and happy. Ain't had a day like this all winter, and where we live that's a big deal. We only have 13 months of winter each year.

All of a sudden the door opened and in came old Frank with his pipe upside down in his mouth, hollering, "Boys, the bulls she's out. Goin' down the road to where those heifers she's at."

As I ran out the door, there was Howie's bicycle layin' on the ground. I grabbed it and headed after the bulls. But I never could, to this day, master that two wheeled mode of travel and I wasn't making too good a time.

Gene ran for the old pickup and got her going, but it was only hitting on three cylinders and a fog of black smoke as he aimed the rig in the direction of those departing bulls.

Wendell headed for the hay shed out south where the horses were. But he never thought about a bridle for the horse, so when he got to the shed where they were shaded up he grabbed a string off a bale of hay, figuring to use it as a bridle. Now the only horse he could catch was Rusty, who was about half broke and didn't rein too good, anyway. Well, Wendell fashioned a loop around Rusty's lower jaw, hopped on and headed north and west after the bulls.

I was wobbling all over that 40 acres trying to master that cockeyed bike, hit a gopher hole and lost a bit of hide. As I got up, I could see Gene right in the middle of those bulls, black smoke pourin' out of that ole pickup. Across the field, I saw this long-legged kid with his white tennis shoes heading those bulls; up against the fence come about 20 large yearling heifers wanting to play too. I gathered up my wheels and head on to help them as best I could.

By this time, Wendell and Rusty had reached the front of the bulls. Now Rusty thought it was a race and wouldn't turn. He ran right on past them. Wendell finally got him turned around at the fence and headed back for the bulls. But old Rusty thought this was fun and ran right through those bulls again, never trying to head them. He raced clear to the south fence, where he finally responded to Wendell's warhoop bridle and started to work cattle. Now we had heifers and bulls all in one bunch.

I gave up my wheels and took out on foot. Say, did you ever cut bulls out of a bunch of heifers while wearing a pair of high heeled riding boots? Don't. It's hard on legs and feet!

Now these young bulls have been in a small lot up to this escapade, with all the hay they can eat and lots of grain. They're plumb fat and ready for the show ring, not at all in shape for such exercise. Boy were they sweating and out of wind.

Finally, we got the big hammer on them and got them headed back to the pen. We got the gate all fastened up tight and headed for the house, a real sight to see: I was pushing my wheels with the chain dragging out behind. Gene left the old pickup in the north corner. Wendell turned Rusty loose and was complaining about saddle sores, though I never could figure how he could get saddle sores when he didn't have a saddle.

Poor old Howie was bellyaching about getting cow manure all over his new white shoes. I could have told him that it wasn't cow manure but bull manure, but I didn't say anything out loud. I just lingered around home the rest of the day, wondering how many calves we'd get two months early next spring.

HE WENT THAT A WAY

Years ago a trip to Missoula, from Ovando, took two days. The roads were either rocks or ruts in the mud and those old Model T's did not travel too fast, so we always stayed overnight and came home the next day.

Now, on this one trip Pop took me along and this was a big trip for a nine or ten year old boy back then. After shopping the first afternoon and spending the night in the Missoula Hotel, we had breakfast in the Grill Cafe next door to the hotel.

Pop seemed to know everyone in town and as we came out on the street he met a guy he knew and they stood there, talking up a storm (Pop sure liked to visit, anybody, any place). I stood there, looking around, when I spotted this lady coming down the street. She was dressed up mighty fine, and had a pair of glasses on a little stick she was holding up in front of her nose. She was strutting along with a little white poodle dog on a leash and this poodle had a haircut that made it look like a miniature African lion. Now, this was summer time and the Grill had an electric screen door to kill the flies. As the poodle came to the door, he trotted over and heisted his leg on it. You should have heard him yap when that juice hit him, and did he leave for parts unknown — he just jerked away from this lady and went northeast.

I'd seen everything and I was laughing my fool head off, but his old girl thought I'd done something to him. Pop and friend, oblivious to everything, are talking and laughing when this lady, who's right beside Pop, turned and slapped him in the face. Pop was surprised and hollered, "What the thunder?" — his favorite cuss words.

The old girl turned and took after her pooch, and after I told Pop and his friend what had happened, they joined in my merriment.

WOBBLY

When we were young kids, each September about the 6th we would go up the North Fork of the Blackfoot fishing. At that time of the season the Dolly Varden (bull trout) would go up the river to spawn. We'd usually camp at Sourdough Flat just above Old Smoke's cabin. Usually there were six of us kids, three of the Reinoehl boys and me and my brothers. And sometimes we'd take a friend or two with us.

The red-bellied native cutthroat were really thick, too, and it was wonderful fly fishing or just a plain hook with a grasshopper for bait.

We always hoped for a frost before we went because it made catching a Prince Albert tobacco can full of hoppers much easier. We'd go out in the meadow where there were lots of hoppers and spread a gunny sack or canvas on the ground. Then, early the next morning before it warmed up, you could raise that sack carefully and pick the hoppers up easy because they were stiff and couldn't fly or hop away.

We didn't mind being the camp cook, but everyone hated to wash dishes, I guess because we hated to get our hands clean (I don't know any other reason). So, we made a deal that the guy who caught the least number of fish on his line at one time had to do dishes.

Sometimes we would have five or six hooks on the same line. When we hooked the first one we'd let him play, dragging the other hooks around. We'd set the hook good on the next one and then they would set the hook on the next one themselves.

When you got no more bites, you'd haul them out slow so as not to lose one — and when you got them in, you'd make sure

The town square of Ovando, Montana, of the era immediately preceding Howard Copenhaver's arrival in the area as a youth. Many of the buildings are now gone.

to have one of the other guys see how many you had or nobody would believe you.

I've seen my brother Gene catch five 12" to 16" trout at the same time in those days but since we couldn't eat them, we'd turn them loose again.

The bull trout would go up the river as far as they could, right up under the falls, which was an 85 foot fall. For about one-half to three-quarters of a mile below the falls, the river goes through a narrow, deep canyon with cliffs several hundred feet high above the water. The water was awfully swift and deep with big, deep holes and huge, big rocks in the middle of the stream and the water rushing around them — real white water. You couldn't wade it; it was too deep and swift, but there was one big pool after another with lots of gravel bars for spawning beds for the bull trout. It was not uncommon to see 15 to 20 spawning at the same time in the same pool.

Well, we'd cut about four inches off the tail of a six- to eight-inch trout and fashion it on a large plain hook so that when

Mountain streams and the outdoors were the setting of many an adventure in Howard Copenhaver's youth. In this photo, from left, are Gene, Howard, Lawrence, Louise and Wendell Copenhaver. Photo courtesy Jon Krutar.

you pulled it through the water, it would dart this way and that much like some of the modern lures do today.

Now these big old males couldn't stand you teasing them in their spawning beds and would fight it, trying to drive it away from their lady love, who was spawning. Finally they'd bite it and you had your hands full landing a big bull in that swift water.

Lots of those we caught were over 30 inches long and weighed from 10 to 20 pounds. You had to be careful when releasing them because they sure had big, sharp teeth. Several times I experienced, when bringing in a cutthroat trout on a fly rod, having a bull trout strike and cut a 15-inch cutthroat right in two. All I had to land, then, was the front end of a nice fish.

It was almost impossible to get the bull trout to take a bait during the peak of their spawning run, but it was really unbelievable fishing. I watched my mother spend three days of fishing on the same rock in the same pool. She even took her

Three Copenhaver boys on the loose in what would come to be known as "Copenhaver Country." From left are Lawrence, Howard and Gene. Photo courtesy Jon Krutar.

lunch and ate it there, never changing pools. She dearly loved to fish one big, deep, blue pool close to camp.

I sure got tied up in fishing didn't I? When I started to tell you about Robley, some relation from Ohio who we took with us one year. I didn't know, or can't remember, how he came to be there. Anyway, he was sure a flatlander, weighing about 160 pounds — real fat and about as clumsy as a cub bear playing baseball.

When you went up the river to the falls to fish the big, deep holes, the canyon was real narrow and there were cliffs right down to the water. You'd crawl around places where you placed your feet on a narrow ledge and dug your fingers into the cliff to hold on as you eased around a bend in the river. And you'd never look at the water because it'd make you dizzy.

At one place the crumbly cliff leveled back from the river

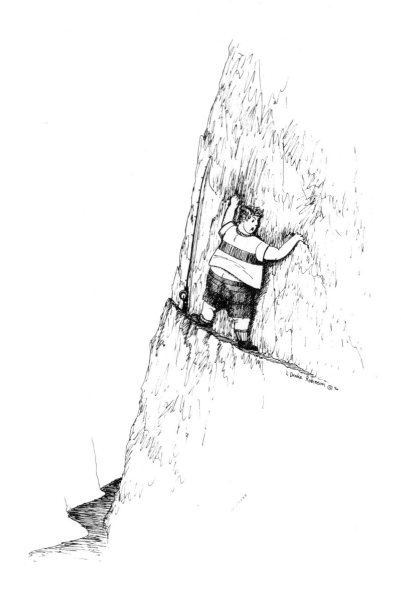

at about an 85 degree slope and there was a nice little ledge angling up across its face and back down to the river — and a beautiful fishing hole. There always were some big old lunkers in that spot!

Now the ledge was from three to four inches wide. You could walk on the side of your feet, leaning over with your hands and hang onto the rock sloping up the mountain. But the rock was crumbly, so you scratched the loose gravel off the ledge before putting weight on your feet.

It was real easy to us guys, but to poor old flatfooted "Wobbly," as we called Robley, it was a tough go. We finally helped him across and fished the upper pools.

On the way back down the river, right out in the middle of this slope Robley looked down at the blue and white water boiling around the rocks and froze solid to that rock wall. We tried everything to get him to come down the ledge but he wouldn't move — or turn loose of the cliff. It looked like we'd have to pry him off, into the river, and then fish him out at the bridge. We couldn't carry him down that ledge because he was too fat. Finally, Frank Reinohl said, "Let's go to camp and leave the so-and-so there. High water will wash him down river next spring."

Down the river we went, all of us except Robley, who was still dug into that cliff, until we were out of sight, around the first bend. We sat down to wait, trying to figure what we're going to do about Robley.

Now, us guys would run up and around that ledge in those days, carrying our fishing pole and a basket of fish. Mebby we didn't have sense enough at that age to be scared. And we didn't have much sympathy for Robley.

Soon we heard a clatter of rocks and, "Don't leave me. Wait for me!" And around the bend came our friend, running and falling over the slick rocks. He'd lost his fishing pole, but we figured it was easier to retrieve that than Robley. He surely never asked to go fishing with us again.

I don't know where he is now, but hope he reads this. I'm sure he is still cussing us with a lot of enthusiasm.

SMILES AND BUTTERMILK

All my life I have probably enjoyed people more than anything else in the whole world. As I look back over the many days of my life I can see myself studying them, trying to figure out what makes them tick, and why we all do some of the things we do. Do you ever wonder the same thing?

Once when I was a small boy, my Dad took me with him to Missoula on a shopping trip. I was sitting in the old Model T truck waiting for him, watching people walk along the street. All of a sudden an elderly man, who was wearing a long overcoat and smoking a pipe, came along. He walked down the street a ways, stopped and stood there for a minute, then turned around and came back past where I was sitting, turned around and went back up the street again. I was wondering why he kept walking back and forth in front of the Missoula Creamery building.

All of a sudden, he stopped right in front of the door, sort of squared his shoulders, and strode into the creamery. I sat there watching to see what would happen next when out came my friend. He stopped in front of our truck, set a gallon of buttermilk down on the sidewalk and then pulled out a pack of Edgeworth tobacco and proceeded to light up his corncob pipe. Out puffed a cloud of smoke. Then he picked up his buttermilk, shoved the jug under his arm with the neck of the bottle pointing down, and took off down the street with a contented look on his face, never noticing that the buttermilk was running out of the jug and into his coat pocket. He was walking along, smiling at the people who in turn are smiling at him and his pocketful of buttermilk.

No one stopped him, not even the dumb kid laughing his

head off sitting in that Old Model T truck. This was at least 69 or 70 years ago and I can still see the pleased look on his face. "Well, I got what I came after."

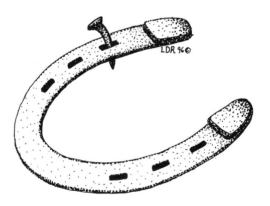

AUNT MINNIE

If you go way back yonder you'll find my family on both sides were quite prolific — got relation scattered all around

Aunt Minnie was from Salt Lake City. Her late husband had been an inventor of mining equipment and left Aunt Minnie quite well fixed. One August she came up to the ranch to spend the rest of the summer. She was young at heart — loved a good time.

We boys were going to a rodeo at Lincoln one day and Dad insisted we take Aunt Minnie.

Mom said, "Don't you boys forget Aunt Minnie. You see she has a good time."

Well, for one, I was far more concerned about whether a gal I knew had a good time than Aunt Minnie.

Now, Aunt Minnie was no slouch when she got dolled up. She was a looker even if we considered her to be a senior citizen and sort of a drag. She showed up ready to go with a black sombrero, brightly flowered shirt, and black riding britches stuffed into Eastern riding boots. You couldn't tell if she was going to a rodeo or a fox hunt, but she looked mighty nice. We were sort of proud of her.

After the rodeo we were at Lambkins where the dance was and beverages were being sold. Everybody was having a great time. This little gal I spoke of and I went out to the car for some serious conversation. We'd no more than got settled in the car when out walked Aunt Minnie and she stopped right in front of the car, and she stood there, looking around. Then out of the bar came old Pop Sanders, an old bronc rider, and he was feeling no pain.

The town of Lincoln, Montana, in earlier days. A fully-paved highway now bisects the town from east to west. (Photo courtesy Jon Krutar)

He sidled up to Aunt Minnie and looked sideways at her. He knew she was a dude but she apparently looked good to him. Aunt Minnie looked up at him.

He said, "Hi ya, Ma."

She looked at him and said, "Hi ya, Pa." Old Pop took her arm and heads back into the bar and dance hall with Aunt Minnie in tow. Our worries were over. She'd have a good time. And I know she did because she only laughed when we told her, later, that we were sitting in the car when she and Pop had introduced themselves to each other.

A few days after this Mom, Dad, Gene, Louise, Aunt Minnie and Lawrence went on a pack trip into the South Fork in the Bob Marshall Wilderness. They planned on going to White River so Joe Murphy, who had cabins at Murphy Flats, told Dad to use his cabins — which they did.

Now Aunt Minnie had a diamond ring that would choke a

cow and she always put it in a glass at night because it bothered her to have it catch on the bed covers. Well, the first night she lost her ring. In the morning it was just gone.

They about wrecked that cabin and shook the bed blankets to pieces but, no ring. Finally, they had to give up. I think she wondered that mebby she hadn't worn it when she left the ranch and just thought she'd taken it off, from habit of doing it, and put it in the glass.

Well, the next night she filled this same glass with water and set it by the head of her bed, and then put her false teeth in it for the night. The next morning the false teeth were gone. Now theare was a panic in camp. No ring. No teeth. Someone was sure in for trouble.

But Mom was cooking breakfast when out of the woodpile came a packrat. It scurried across the floor and, for us, the mystery was solved. Packrats love shiny things. They pack them to their nest and save them — and we were sure the rat had grabbed Aunt Minnie's goodies.

Next came the search for the packrat's nest and everybody was in on this one, including Aunt Minnie, all tears and no teeth. Finally, out from under the cabin came Gene with an ear-to-ear grin on his face. In his hand he grasped a fat diamond ring, plus a set of false teeth that needed a chance at some cleanser and a brush.

GREEN AS GRASS

I stopped in at "Trixi's," the local dispenser of cool drinks, the tail end of hunting season last fall just to see how the hunters were doing and, plainly, just to shoot the bull.

As I walked up to the bar where some friends sat bending their elbows, around the bar came this guy and slapped me on the back saying, "Howard it has been many years since I last saw you. I was a sixteen-year-old kid back in the summer of 1963 the last time we saw each other. Sure good to see you."

He continued, "My dad, uncle and a friend stayed all night at your place and packed into the Danaher and Big Prairie on a fishing trip. Don't you remember when you caught up to us with your party down in the Basin? I cut you some wood when you set up camp across the creek from us?"

"I'm sorry but I don't," I said.

After he reminded me that I'd loaned them two pack mules, it all came to light. Here's how it all came about.

This guy had called me asking to use our corrals and leave their truck and car at the ranch while they were gone on a week's pack trip. I said sure it was okay. They had hay to feed their own stock. Well, when they arrived they had four saddle horses and three pack animals. It looked okay to me, at a glance, as they were starting to manti up their pack for a good start the next morning.

The boys at the ranch and I were busy the next morning, getting ready for a big pack trip the following day, when here came this guy, who asked, "Howard, do you have time to give us some advice on packing our stuff?"

I said, "Sure," and went around the saddle shed where they

One of the earlier locations of the famed "Trixi's Saloon" in Ovando, which now is located adjacent to Highway 200 at the northeastern edge of the town, was this building on the town square — which currently houses a museum.

were getting packed up. Advice was all they wanted, but what they needed was a whole string of mules and a packer with a sense of humor and lots of time. There was stuff scattered all over the place, and some packs made up that resembled bales of hay with one string broken — a packer's nightmare.

After I'd gone through this stuff, thrown out what they didn't need, and wrapped up the packs, they still needed two more pack animals. Well, I loaned them two old mules and the rigging, loaded them up and sent them up the trail. I didn't worry about the two mules as I knew they were old and smart enough; if the going got too rough, they'd take a powder and come home.

Three days later when we pulled into Camp Creek down in the basin, right across the creek splashed this sixteen-year-old kid, volunteering his help. We got the cook outfit set up and he said, "What can I do now?"

"Things are in pretty good shape. I'm going to cut some wood for Dutch to cook supper with."

He said, "I'll get you some. I just cut a big pile." And across the creek he went.

I picked up the axe and went to look for a dry log to split up. When I came back with an armful of dry wood and some pitch kindling, here was my friend with a pile of wood in front of the stove. Now, in the area there is a lot of young jackpine about ten feet tall. He had spent his day chopping them into stove lengths — all green jackpine. You couldn't burn them with a blow torch, let alone in a sheepherder's stove.

I lit some pitch kindling and filled the stove with dry wood, and shoved the green wood off to the side. Old Dutch set the coffee pot on the stove and as I stepped back this kid said, "Don't you like my wood?"

Dutch put on that crooked grin and, with his eyes twinkling out from under his old hat, said, "Kid we like your wood fine but our stove don't. Let me tell you something, son. If'n you're going to warm up a kettle or your best girl, you'd better start with dry wood."

Now, after 33 years, this kid, a grown man, still thanked me for what he'd learned, bought me a drink and was the brunt of the laughter that afternoon at Trixi's.

ME AND THAT SADDLE

I don't know how many words I've written over the last few years. There have been hundreds and thousands of them, some misspelled and some not. And there were so many in the wrong place that I made little balls out of them and threw them at the wastebasket. And, like all good basketball players, I've got about a 30% average at hitting the bucket.

In those words, I have tried to show what a great life this has been with such great folks. Now I'm going to give a new slant on some of the tracks between the sunshine.

I was at a rodeo at a dude ranch one time and while the calf roping was going on, several of us bronc riders felt we were in need of a bit of libation to beef up our courage, so's to speak. One guy had a jug of old Scoop Moore's best moonshine, so we went into the tack room to have a round.

Hanging on the peg on the wall was this beautiful ladies' sidesaddle. It was a beauty; English leather padded seat and swell, a beautiful piece of leather work — and the pride of Mrs. Weisel who owned the Circle W Ranch.

Sure enough, I got my big mouth going and said, "Boys, I'd sure like to cinch that rig on a good bronc and come out of that chute just once."

A voice sounded off right behind me and it ain't one of the boys. It was Mrs. Weisel and she said, "Cowboy, I got fifty bucks just to see you do it once."

I said, "You're on," and offered her some of our beverage as I had it in my hand. She accepted and out the door I went with this beautiful rig over my arm.

Howard Copenhaver and saddle during his heyday as an outfitter.

They shoved a big hammer-headed pony into the chute and we screwed that little rig to his back; he sort of looked like an elephant with a frog on his back.

I slid down into place sort of easy like and tucked my right leg around the horn, stuck my toe under the left leg and hooked my left spur deep in that cinch. Then I nodded to the gate handler and we had the arena and all the big sky to ourselves — just me and that hammer-headed old pony.

Now he may not have been a national finals champ, but he sure knew I wasn't supposed to be up there in his middle. And we were doing just fine when the rigging in that saddle snapped right at the top of one of his high humps. That rotten old goat left me and my sidesaddle up there in the sky, all alone.

Well, what could I do? I turned over once but couldn't shake loose from that little rig holding my legs together like a hobble skirt. When we hit the ground the saddle was still there and I was on my head. I can still feel that wallop that saddle gave me; mebby it was mad because I broke the cinch.

My advice is, don't try this one, boys. It's only fun for the guys sittin' on the fence, but I limped home with fifty bucks — and in the 1930's that felt good.

Now, this brings about some more memories of the Weisel family and our connections. It was about that same time in the 1930's that a guy with a goofy moustache over in Europe came into fame and power doing good for lots of people, but as it seems to happen so often, he forgot the good. They called him Adolph.

Anyway, he sure had France and England with their tails in a wringer and hollering, "Uncle." Yeah, I said, "Uncle." This little short, fat guy with a big cigar puffed out a cloud of blue smoke and Uncle Sam said, "I hear you Winston. We'll be there." Someone waved a flag under my nose and I joined the Navy. I was going to help them make that landing at Anzio, or in France. Then, out of the clear blue, came this guy "Tojo" and I was off to throwing lead at the Japanese.

Well, they didn't take to this very well and threw some back. I got in the way of some of it. It seems like I didn't move quite fast enough and ended up in the hospital in New Caledonia.

Uncle Sam figured he ought to tell someone about it, but didn't say what was really wrong and some people believed I was a casualty or was dead — though the Navy and I knew better. They sent me back to duty aboard the old "Maryland," a battle wagon that was getting repaired in Pearl Harbor.

I still wasn't in very good shape, hardly walking around, when the commanding doctor called me up to his cabin and said, "Don't you do anything but walk around and I'll have you state-bound to a hospital in 'Frisco within a few days."

The second day I was aboard the Maryland, I was piped to the quarterdeck. I said to myself, "Mebby this is a start for home sweet home."

But when I got there, who was there to greet me but this tall, lanky George Weisel, who had about all the gold from Fort Knox on his shoulders and cap. He is the son of Mrs. Weisel, who owned the Circle W Ranch in Montana. He was shocked to see me alive as he heard I was feeding fish somewhere in the South

Pacific. He'd come aboard to see if he could send any of my belongings to Marg and get the particulars of what had happened.

He turned to the officer of the day and asked if I could have liberty the next day as he wanted to take me to lunch with a group of his associates on Honolulu.

The next day I met him at this hotel and when we got to the dining room, the table was lined with the top brass of the Pacific area. Now I'll tell you what, I was embarrassed. I felt like a burro in a flock of pretty sheep because I was a poor little Boatswain's Mate Second Class.

But, the years have rolled by and George and I still see each other. He has been retired many years and shows up whenever I'm shoeing horses and mules for an outfitter in Missoula. He just stands there and watches me shoe, trim and nail on those horseshoes. When we quit for the day, he'd go home.

Now this went on for several years until one day when I hit the horseshoe nail with my hammer, and the nail was bent over flat against the horse's foot. George jumped up from where he was sitting and said, "I'm going home. I've sat here and waited all this time just to see you bend a nail."

And, just a couple of days ago, just as we were getting into the truck to come home from this same place, up drove a car and out stepped old George. "Going to shoe horses today?" he asked.

"Nope," I said, "We're all done, George. You must be getting old. It takes you too long to do anything anymore." We had a good visit and a few laughs. (May we meet many times again.)

While I'm on this Navy bit, I should tell you about an Ensign who was assigned to our division as a Junior Officer. Now any man who has lived to breathe fresh air has heard about the no-good officers in any armed forces of the world. But some of the best men I have ever known have had a good supply of gold on their shoulders; there were some dandies, just like in all walks of life.

We'd been three years "down under" in the Coral Sea, Truk Island, Eniwetok, and had been involved in many more invasions when this lad came aboard, dropped off by a seaplane. Every morning at quarters he gave a lengthy speech about how all of us on the ship were disposable and should feel it an honor to die for our country. All of us "old-timers" had all we could take of him — we'd seen it all, from Pearl Harbor to Borneo, and he was fresh out of cow college.

Now, in our ranks was a great guy, a big Italian who stood six feet four inches and cut in at 250 to 280 pounds, just a swell guy. One morning came along and this fellow just couldn't take it anymore; he walked out of lineup to the "Jug Butt," as we called the new officer, and grabbed him by the front of his coat, lifted him up with one hand until his feet were dangling and said, "Sir, I respect your rank and uniform, but we'll dispense with the sermon as of now."

He dropped "Jug Butt" and stepped back in line, standing at attention. Jug Butt said, "Carry on men. You are dismissed."

A few days later we had an air attack, high level bombing. One bomb exploded right off the port side and right under our gun tube. There was some slight damage done by shrapnel — nothing to write home about — but when we secured from General Quarters and checked noses, we were short one Jug Butt. A search was set in order and a destroyer was called to go back on our wake and look for a man who might have been blown overboard due to the concussion. Nobody was found. After some time had passed, a sailor said, "I hear a noise like somebody calling and it's coming from that big ventilator by gun tube four." A search revealed Jug Butt, wrapped around the vent tube underneath the cover bell.

Now this bell cover was welded to the tube and only four inches off the deck. How a man could force his body under it I don't know, but in his fright Jug Butt had done just that. He was badly bruised, that's all. The next morning, a seaplane taxied up alongside our ship and Jug Butt was put aboard. I guess the Captain didn't have as much use for him as we did.

Then we had this big man nicknamed "Chief," a Blackfoot Indian from Browning, Montana, who was a Gunner's Mate First

Class. He was a three-hashmark sailor, meaning he had 12 years in. He was gunner's mate on an old British Pom-Pom back on the quarterdeck, which was also was my first battle station when I went aboard ship.

The Pom-Pom was an anti-aircraft gun that, when fired, sounded just like it said — "Pom-Pom." And it was a good close range, anti-aircraft gun. On the end of the barrel was a flash-plate, something like a steel horn to keep the muzzle flash from being seen from a distance.

Well, we were under air attack one night right after they'd come out with the metallic fused projectile and these shells would explode when they came close to metal, creating a shrapnel effect. However, sometimes, if the fuse was not set just right, they'd explode when they left the barrel, inside of the flash plate, and blow that flash plate all over the area.

This one night, Chief was sitting on a ready box off to the side, watching the show, when a flash plate blew. A long sliver of it flew through the air, red hot, and hit the ready box where Chief sat, and it slid along and, just like a big safety pin, pinned his two buttocks together.

Up he jumped, running down the deck, smoke pouring out from both hams with the hot iron sticking out both sides. He was hollering at the top of his voice, "I'm wounded, I'm wounded!"

They pulled out the flash plate sliver and I never saw Chief sit on that ready box again. The ship doctor said, "Best job of cauterizing I've ever seen."

You know, some of us are just plain dumb and others are just ignorant, but education really comes easy if the forces behind it are strong enough. To show you what I mean, consider that when I went aboard ship, I didn't know an admiral from a mess cook. Uniforms meant that an officer paid a lot more for his glad rags than a plain old swab jockey, but I knew you should follow orders from an officer, but who was what just didn't ring a bell with me. I'd just come out of the hills of old Montana and I had my own ideas of what was what.

The first day aboard I was given a paint pot and a brush,

along with another boot (sailor recently arrived from boot camp), and showed a big gun turret to paint. I was told, "Finish it or no liberty."

Now I knew a little gal in Seattle I hadn't seen for quite a spell, so I sure wasn't going to miss that first liberty. Everything was going fine and we only had a tail hatch to paint when they blew sweepers — that's a call over the loudspeaker system that means that you drop what you're doing and grab a broom and help sweep all decks forward and aft.

I said to my new buddy, "Take the paint to the paint locker and I'll finish this and be right down."

I was slappin' that paint on the hatch when down the ladder came these black shoes and blue legs. I stepped back to let this officer down. It was our division officer, a Lieutenant Commander. He said, "Ain't you a sweeper?"

I said, "Yes."

He said, "Why are you standing here?"

I said, "I'm finishing this job. What's it look like?"

He said, "So you're one of those wise ----- -----."

I just wasn't used to being called such names, so I busted him in the mouth, knocking out two front teeth.

He spit blood and said, "Report to your division."

I took the paint and brush to the locker, showered, shaved, picked up my liberty card and went on the beach — with everyone telling me I was due for a court-martial and the brig. Well, the next morning at quarters, the First Class Boatswain read from his paper: "Copenhaver S 2/C step forward." I did and this Lieutenant Commander said, "Due to your show of insubordination, you are assigned Captain of the Head in the Second Division for the total of one year."

If you don't have any idea what that means, here it is: I had the honor of cleaning the toilet for 60 to 70 men for a year. It sure didn't put any chevrons on my arm regardless of the title. I had to ask what it meant but I found out.

Now the Chief's quarters were right forward of the head. I finally got smart and would run the chipping hammer on that wall at night, chipping paint, and then paint it again the next day. Those old Chiefs finally came to my rescue; they got me removed from Captain of the Head to the Sail Locker, which was good duty.

I finally became good friends with that Lieutenant Commander and asked him why he gave me a general. His reply was, "I was wrong. Any man that would take what I called you and not strike back, I don't want under my command." He pushed me up to 2/c Boatswain in one year and stood behind me. He was really one great guy.

PATCHES THE QUEEN

Way back in 1962, a group of dude ranchers and outfitters were talking about advertising. Suddenly, Howard Kelsey of the Nine Quarter Circle Ranch out of Gallatin Gateway, Montana, got the floor. He said, "What we ought to do is go East with a train load of horses and pack mules and parade some of those big cities." Everybody laughed and talked about it but no one realized what would come of such a suggestion.

Now, my friend, Howard Kelsey, was not a guy who warmed a chair after getting an idea that sounded good. He got around a campfire up on the Taylor Fork one night with a group of influential men from New York, from Great Falls and Bozeman, Montana, and a plan was born and did it grow! Meeting after meeting, committees, board meetings, on and on. Finally, the Montana Centennial Commission was formed.

Then came the work of raising funds, signing up people to go. And buying a long train and clearing it with railroad companies to use their engines and tracks, plus arrangements with city governments to parade on their streets, advertisements with newspapers, radio stations and television people, and for hotels and banquet space. It goes on forever, but we were expected and very successful. We ended up with parlor cars for the horses and mules, exhibit cars, Pullman cars and dining cars — all owned by the Centennial Commission. Then came the volunteers to help get it ready and work on the trip a total of over 300 people from their teens to the oldest man in Montana, Native Indian dancers and 175 head of horses and mules. There was also plenty of Old Yellowstone whisky, though I never saw a drunk person on the 30-

day trip through 14 of the major cities east of the Mississippi River.

We had exhibition cars with the art from many of the great Montana artists and $1,000,000 in Montana gold, silver and other native gems on display — all because of an old cowboy's dream he wasn't afraid to tell people about.

At the first meeting, I opened my big mouth and said, "Get it off the ground and I'll put up the first check." Well, as you guessed by now, me and Marg were right in the middle of it with two saddle horses and four mules packing kitchen, duffel and meat and antlers up and down the streets. And this is where Patches, my pinto mule, came in. But first, a few things happened along the rail, not the trail I was used to riding.

Now, we had to train all this stock to get used to cars, people, and plenty of noises. They'd never heard a train whistle in the hills of old Montana. Five other guys and I ended up with 46 head of mules and horses at the fairgrounds in Missoula, Montana. The people of Missoula helped us a lot, honking their horns, revving their motors and yelling at us to get out of their way. The police were very cooperative, too. They allowed us to train on the race track and rodeo arena or we couldn't have got it done.

After we got some working pretty good, we'd go out on the streets right down Main Street. Sometimes it was fine, other times the public didn't act as if they enjoyed our show.

One day, Herb Toelke said, "I'm going to hitch all six up today. I think my lead team is shaped up good enough for the streets."

Now, he was driving six head of 16-hand, 1,500-pound colts pulling a big Tallyho Stage. This team is well-matched sorrels with lots of spirit. We got all lined out, made a turn around the race track and headed down the main street for town traffic. All went well till we hit the Higgins Avenue bridge. Right in the middle of the bridge, Herb met a bicycle ridden by a guy whose big, flappy coat was waving in the breeze. These old ponies hadn't ever seen a bicycle before, let alone a live one waving a coat right under their noses. Before you could say "Jack Robinson," those

Patches the Queen at work in the high country of Montana.

ponies jackknifed and Herb lost the show! Well, the team, Tallyho and Herb were crossways on the bridge, with car horns honking, people screaming advice and a few unprintable sayings at him.

We finally got the nags straightened out, into motion and finished our tour without any further incident.

Just one more. We were in Baltimore, Maryland, parading down the street with hundreds of people on each side enjoying the show when another incident occurred. I was leading my pack mules, all loaded and doing nice, when just like a flash, the pack on my third mule back in the string turned under his belly. Luckily, Marg was able to hold my saddle horse and head mule while I repacked my mule as the rest of the parade went around us. I had lots of volunteer help those on the sidewalk, but was it embarrassing at the time — a hotshot in cold water.

But, back on line with my story in regard to getting ready for the big trip. We had to get all that stock used to parading and also legged up so they wouldn't get stiff walking on all the cement streets ahead of them. Also, they had their long Montana winter hair on them and we had to blanket them to get them to shed it off so they would look nice and slick and clean.

Now, don't you know Old Man Winter changed his mind and turned the temperature down to 28 to 30 degrees below zero. Those horses needed, and grew, hair. We then had but one choice, to clip the hair off with hair clippers. We'd throw a horse, someone would sit on its head, and we'd tie all four feet and go to work. In about four days the job was done. We sure had a pile of horse hair and some mighty sore spots where we didn't move fast enough to miss a iron-shod hoof aimed with mulish accuracy.

Next came the vet deal. Each animal had to have a series of shots for who knows what kind of diseases. Well, we contracted a vet to do all of this and clear the papers for each state we would visit on the tour. This old doc knew his business but old Patches, after the first shot, hated that guy. I could take the needle, go into her stall and give her a shot and all she'd do was jump a little, but if the vet showed up she'd kick that stall to pieces. It got so that the day he was to give another shot, I'd tie her to a hitchrack outside before he came. She got so she knew the sound of his truck and would start to raise Cain before he got close to her.

One day I didn't tie her up in time. The vet showed up and Patches was loose in the box stall with her blanket still strapped on her. She heard his car stop out front and she started kicking the walls and door of the stall. Off flew the door and out came Patches, headed anyplace away from there.

Well, Freddie Deschamps has just gotten his four-horse team hooked up to the hay wagon and he was climbing on to give them a workout on the track when round the barn came Patches on a run, tail and head high and that blanket flapping in the air. Away went Freddie's four-horse team. He made a grab for his lines, got only one, and hauled back, hollering, "Whoa!" They kept going, but he turned them into the race track gate and from then on it was a race — with no holds barred. Those four old ponies decided to leave the country, and right behind came Patches and her blanket.

L. Drake - Robinson © 96

Poor old Freddie; they lost him at the gate. Some thoughtful guy drove a truck across the gate and the race was on.

First they lost the rack and hind wheels, then a front wheel that couldn't dodge a post. By then, the team's spirit was ebbing and the sweat running and the horses kegged up in the far corner of the track, Patches had lost her blanket, and the dust finally settled. We gathered up the pieces and it was decided that what Freddie really needed was a new wagon, a few bandaids, and a good stiff drink to bring heart and mind back together again.

Finally, we got them all in shape and loaded on the train and headed for Billings, Montana, to pair up with the rest of the crew from the east side of the state.

When we unloaded at Billings, everybody wanted to know how we had gotten our stock to shed off and look so nice and slick. So there we went again — clipping horses and trimming tails. Didn't have enough time to finish before we left, so we completed the job in Omaha, Nebraska, before the first parade.

Oh yeah, there was an older bachelor from up by Red Lodge who had brought his Palomino saddle horse, long haired and dirty, right out of the hills. I don't think that horse had ever had a curry comb or brush run over his hide. He looked terrible, but the guy wouldn't let us clip him. Said he was fine. We tried to get him to use a curry and brush because his horse was dirty, but he said, "Never owned a comb! No use for one." One evening we sheared this nag. Well, the next morning this old boy threw his saddle on him, jerked up the cinch, stepped back and looked at his horse. In a loud, booming voice he shouts to the world, "Now that's the way a horse oughta look. Haven't you guys ever heard of a curry comb and brush?"

One of the outrider's with the Indian wagon (named Fred) had a beautiful Appaloosa saddle horse. He had a perfectly spotted blanket of black and white spots over his hips. Now Fred's wife, a redhead with fire enough for two women, was riding an old white horse. Everyone else had matched horses of the same color. We had working with us three young cowboys with more spirit than good sense, Howie, Walt and Gary, who figured this didn't make the rest of our outfit look so good. So, one night they got some India ink and made an Appy out of the white horse. But they didn't stop at that — they drew tepees and Indian sign language all over old Whitey. When Fred and wife came to saddle up for the parade next morning, you should have heard Fred. Was he wild! But due to the compliments they received after the parade, his lovely lady sort of liked it. Fred's complaints wouldn't have made any difference anyway, because you couldn't brush or wash off those signs; any change now had to wait for new hair to grow in. And, until he reads this, Fred has never known who performed this miracle.

After the show in Omaha, we went to Cincinnati, Ohio. Now, the Indian dances were a high spot in the whole show and people were constantly after the dancers to perform on television programs and in night spots. Also, every city we hit was invited to bring the grade school kids to tour the Centennial Train exhibition cars free of charge. So here would come a big line of kids, with a teacher on each end to kind of keep them together, one line after another, all day long, going through the display cars.

One day we were parked at the Central Station in Cincinnati, a huge place. People had to come through a big lobby, going and coming from the cars, and it was a busy place because trains were in use back then.

On this one particular day, the Indian dancers had put on a show somewhere uptown and they were dressed in all the Indian finery, tomahawks and all, and could they dance! Kenny Left Hand was a big, young man and full of the devil. Just as Kenny came into the lobby from the street in all his Indian finery, the school kids were headed out and Kenny let out a warhoop or two and took after these kids, waving his tomahawk, dancing, with all the little bells on his wrists and ankles ringing. You should have seen those kids go.

There was no place to hide, but there was a string of ladies and men toilets along the far wall and the doors flew open and the screaming kids dashed in. Out, just as fast, came women shaking down their dresses and men zipping up their pants. What a riot.

One little boy fell right in the middle of the station. Kenny danced up to him with his tomahawk raised in the air. This kid jumped to his knees, put his hands under his chin, sort of prayer-like, and screamed, "Please no, Mr. Indian." Kenny gently picked him up and gave him some feathers and an Indian headband, and the show was all over. I'll bet that kid still has those feathers and headband.

Then we were ready for Kansas City, where some of the young cowboys went looking for that gal a guy had written the song about, "Kansas City Kitty," but I don't think they ever found her.

By this time, we had all the kinks and troubles worked out and had a very professional parade going. We were down to getting shaped up and on the streets almost on the minute, with everyone pulling together in a big team.

We were moving down the main street, Marg and I with our mules, when out of a barber shop raced this guy with the cloth

The Montana Centennial Train.

around his neck and white lather on one side of his face, hollering my name at the top of his voice. We couldn't stop so we simply waved, and wonder who he was. When we got back to the station, I was being paged over the loudspeaker system, and was given a phone number. I called and it was a former guest, a hunter I'd had on an elk hunt a few years before. He had been having a shave and haircut when, through the barbershop window, he saw old Patches. He had just jumped out of the chair and ran out the door. "I knew you wouldn't be far away from Patches," he said. And was he surprised! He hadn't heard of our parading in Kansas City. And he never did tell me what the barber had said about his hasty exit from the chair.

We moved on to Louisville, Kentucky, where we made our first parade without freezing.

One of our former guests and her mother picked Marg and I up at the station and drove us to "Calumet Farms," home of Bull Lee, the world-famous racehorse and sire. It was great to see the magnificent animal, even though he was old at the time. You could see royalty showing in his actions and blood lines.

Then we went on to Frankfort, Kentucky, and up into the governor's office, where they made me an honorary "Kentucky Colonel," long Kentucky rifle and all. And, as we were leaving the room we met a group of dignitaries ushering in Montana's Governor Tim Babcock to accept the same honor. I have held it over poor Tim's head ever since — I was made a Kentucky Colonel before him. He was second choice.

Look out Washington, D.C., we thought, when we got to the nation's capitol, where we were really treated like royalty. The city came out and put on a big banquet in our honor. It was great. But before the banquet, a few things came up.

We paraded down Pennsylvania Avenue and around the circle at the White House. The sidewalks were lined with dignitaries; on the steps stood President Lyndon Johnson and others. Montana senators and representatives were right down at the street edge on the sidewalk, greeting us as each unit passed. When your unit came even with them, you simply paused for a minute to pay your respects to them.

When a unit would stop, out would step Senator Mike Mansfield, who reached out and shook hands and called everyone by his or her first name. Now, I was thinking that this old boy sure knew a lot of Montanans on a first name basis when I realized that the guy standing beside him had a paper and pen and was cuing him along with the names.

Right in front of Marg and I were Herb Toelke and the Tallyho. As Herb stopped his six-horse hitch, Mike stepped up on the loading step and shook Herb's hand, and said, "Good to see you again, Herb." Herb gathered up his lines and, with that big booming voice, said to his shotgun rider, "Who the hell was that S.O.B.? Never saw him before in my life."

As he drove away, you should have heard the people laugh, clear up to President Johnson. Herb was great but never ceased to open his mouth and stick his foot in.

The parade went swell. No trouble at all that day so everyone was ready for the banquet that night. With us were Bonny Jo, Miss Montana, and Kitty Quigley, Miss Montana Centennial, who led the parade and appeared on television and radio stations, singing and answering questions about Montana. Now some gals just go along with the show, but not Kitty. You never knew what she'd do, but you could bet it would be different.

When we got settled down at our tables that evening in a huge banquet hall, Kitty was at our table. Dignitaries were giving their "One-two-three-testing" at the microphone and everybody was chatting, paying little attention to what was being said. Suddenly, a loud voice boomed out over the intercom, "Ladies and Gentlemen, the President of the United States." And in walked President Johnson, down a winding stairs to the podium. Everyone rose to their feet, but not before Kitty jumped up, gave a cowboy holler and jerked out her two six-shooters, which were loaded with blanks, and shot into the air. Now, you never saw so many Secret Service men in your life. They were all over Kitty immediately and had her guns — just about scared poor Kitty to death. The crowd went wild laughing and President Johnson thanked her for

Margaret and Howard Copenhaver in New York City during the adventure they shared as part of the Montana Centennial Train group.

the Montana greeting, gave a short speech and left. I'll tell you what! Kitty sure put the cowboy trimmings on that high toned affair.

When we first started the real planning of this trip, Mr. Moses of the New York World Fair board offered us space for two years for our exhibit cars and asked us to lead the opening day parade to start the World's Fair of 1964, which we did. This, by itself, was quite an accomplishment but we also thought it was a great way to finish a month-long circle of parades and shows.

The Centennial Train exhibit was left in New York with a crew to tend it and we've never forgotten the volunteers who finished our big show in New York. A corral of poles was built and a few cattle were left to have on exhibit. One cow had a calf while New Yorkers, television men and women, newspapers and all watched and enjoyed nature from Montana at its best.

Then we were headed west, looking for mountains and home, and by this time you are wondering why this story is entitled "Patches, the Queen." Well, here it is. This mule, Patches, was a pinto, tall, well put together and had a character of her own. She could get into more trouble in five minutes than you could get her out of in an hour, but she was a good pack mule.

While we were on this tour, the Ralston Purina Company donated a horse ration to feed our stock. It was ground up alfalfa, corn, oats and barley compressed into pellets with molasses as binder, making it sweet and palatable. We fed no hay so the stock lacked bulk in their diet and they were always hungry and craved grass. When we were in Clarksville, Virginia, where there was grass between the tracks, we tied the horses on a line along the parlor cars to let them stay out in the fresh air during the night. One morning when we went to water and feed them, Patches was gone. How she got rid of her halter I'll never know. But, after a search around the train cars and puffing engines, we found the old gal across the yard, peacefully grazing between the tracks.

When we were at our last stop before heading home and were short on food for the horses, someone showed up with a truck-load of hay. We scattered it along the picket line so the stock

L. Drake-Robinson 96©

could eat while they were tied to the line. The Shetlands were tied right next to my mules, all eating peacefully. Some kids, with their mothers watching close by, were sitting there, petting the Shetland's heads. One kid had a wooly head of hair, kind of a big Afro haircut. Well, he must have been in Patches' way because she just reached over took a mouthful of that pile of hair, gave the kid a shake and threw him out of the way.

Up jumped the kid, running toward his mother, screaming, "I was bitten by a mule." But that was as far as the incident went; the kid seemed to be pleased that old Patches had picked him instead of some other kid. As for Patches, she went right on munching that big bite of Afro hay. No pain, no strain.

On our way home, we got our first glimpse of those Crazy Mountains as we rolled into Billings, Montana, and we were anxious to be home. But the west-side-bound cars headed for Missoula were sidetracked and, after about three hours, a switch engine hooked up to the tail end of a slow freight headed west and we were once again on our way. We didn't get far when we realized that right in front of us was about five carloads of pigs. By then, we had lost our fancy parlor cars, so were riding with the baggage and the horse cars. Boy, you should have smelled the fresh air that came from the pig cars ahead. What a ride.

When we hit the Continental Divide out of Butte, those horses and mules started braying and whinnying and continued to do so until they were unloaded at the Missoula stockyards. How they knew they were home I don't know, but they did. We turned them loose in the stockyards and they started to run. And they ran and ran and ran, until each owner had loaded their stock on trucks, and headed home.

As for me, the memory of that trip lingers. It was a great trip with great people, many new friends and experiences no one else will ever have.

Thank you, Howard Kelsey, for dreaming. And Patches for some great memories.

THE COMMENTATOR

Many years ago we had an organization called "Western Montana Outfitters." It was the first such organization in the state. We'd been running for a number of years and most of the outfitters and dude ranchers west of the Continental Divide belonged, a fairly large group. Each year we would have a convention the first week in December, always at the Florence Hotel in Missoula.

This particular year we had several outfitters and dude ranchers from the eastern side of the divide that wanted to join our organization. We both needed their support and wanted their friendship and help in state legislative business, so we were going all out to make this a real convention. In other words, we were really going to put on our Sunday clothes.

On previous occasions, we'd always gotten some local lad as a featured speaker, but someone came up with the idea of having a real pro this time. Now, one of the boys and just come from Billings, Montana, and he said this famous commentator from Los Angeles was to speak in Billings just a day or two before our convention, and that probably we could get him to stop by and do the honors.

Somebody contacted him and arrangements were made for us to pick him up in Butte, Montana, and for $500.00 he'd give us his best. Well, we got hold of old Jimmy from the 320 Ranch and he said he'd pick him up in Butte, as he was coming over to Missoula anyway, for the 120-mile ride from Butte to Missoula.

We had it in the papers and over Missoula's only radio station, KGVO, and gave the famous commentator a good advertisement — invited the public to dinner, etc. We really set it up nice.

Well, when Jim showed up with our speaker, Jim got me and old Herb in the corner and said, "You guys sure got your tail in the door. This guy is not only balmy, he's just plain nuts."

Old Hobnail Tom said, "Oh, he can't be that bad. He's worldly known."

Well, in less than two hours he had all the ladies scared to get close to him and two of us men went every place with him to keep him in line. We had a big crowd at dinner that night and his speech was terrible, nothing pertaining to the industry, state or nation. He thought he was a joke teller, but they were so foul no lady or gentleman could appreciate them.

After dinner and at the cocktail party, someone said, "We've got to do something with his guy."

I said, "Come with me. Let's get him so drunk he passes out." I figured this wouldn't be hard, considering his appetite for booze.

"Good," said Jim, and headed for his room to get a fifth of whiskey. I went for some ice. I got three of those little plastic buckets you haul ice to your room in, put some ice in each one and when Jim came back we poured about a pint of whiskey in one bucket and thinned it down with vodka and lemon juice. In the others, we had ginger ale and water.

We went back to the cocktail party and I said to this guy, who I'll simply call Joe, "Joe, we want to make you an honorary member, but all candidates have to drink a 'Rocky Mountain Cocktail' with us before we can accept them as members." He seemed very pleased when Jim and I raised our buckets to toast him. Now, he went after his bucket like a camel who hadn't seen water in three weeks. We kept patting him on the back and tipping our buckets in his honor. Well, in about 30 minutes Mr. World Famous Commentator is out like a turned-off lamp. He fell out of his chair. Four of us picked him up and packed him off to his room. He was just like carrying a 2 x 12 plank. We threw him on his bed and left him.

But, we sure had a time waking him up the next day, about 3 in the afternoon, so we could get him to the airport by 4 o'clock. I'll tell you, he looked like the last rose of summer. As he headed up the ramp to the plane, still sort of shaky, he turned and said, "I've always heard of your Montana hospitality. It was great, but I can stand no more."

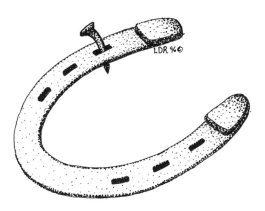

LADY LUCK SMILES

I walked into Trixi's one afternoon and up came this good-looking babe. She threw her arms around me and hollered, "Howard, it's been so long since I last saw you. This is wonderful." Everybody's looking at me and I'm sure enough dumbfounded. Then I see a smiling face grinning at me. It's Guy Clatterbuck, old Ted Clatterbuck's young son.

I said to the gal, "Mebby I should know you, but I don't. You look familiar but I see lots of pretty girls that look familiar. Mebby I'm just wishin'."

She said, "I'm Kay, Ted's oldest daughter. It's so good to see you."

Well we all chatted awhile and finally it came down to stories of long ago. Now Ted, her dad, was the best storyteller I've ever run into, so now I'm writing another one about "Ted the Horse Trader" (Page 109 in "They Left Their Tracks). This happened up at Ted's place just south of Ronan, Montana, on a sunny, summer day.

Ted said, "Come with me. I want you to look at a real horse. He bucks a little they say, but has a rein on him just like silk. If I can buy him right I know where I can make some good money on him. Know just the right guy to sell him to. He's got a big ranch and needs good cow horses."

Now, at this time a $100 bill would buy just about any horse you wanted. You could get good geldings for $75.00. We headed for this old boy's ranch and Ted said, "I sure hope we get there before he rides this pony cause sometimes they won't buck after the first ride in the morning. This is the way it is with lots of spoiled ranch horses. Once they know you can ride them they just won't waste the effort till the next morning."

When we drove up, this old pony was standing in the corral munching hay. His back had wet spots on it and it sure hadn't rained last night, so we knew he'd been ridden that morning. But he sure enough was all horse; you could see at the first look. Had a lot of thoroughbred in him, 16 hands tall, trimmed legged and 1,200 pounds of body on straight legs and feet, blood bay in color and a white strip down his face. He needed to have his tail and mane trimmed, but sure would turn the head of a good horseman anyplace.

Ted and this guy talked a bit and the guy said, "Want to ride him?"

"Yeah, I'd sure like to," Ted said, as he hauled his saddle out of the truck. When he got the horse saddled, old Ted swung up and took a deep seat, kinda nudged the horse off center and headed for the gate.

Now that old pony let a squall out of him and went in the air, high and crooked. Ted was sitting up there looking good when all of a sudden they parted company and he stretched old Ted full length on the road, then headed back to the hay pile.

This guy went over, gathered the reins, and led the horse back to where Ted was trying to get some wind back in his lungs.

"Want to try another sittin'," he said to Ted. Ted was rubbing some spots that ain't needed rubbing before. He just grinned and said, "Sure."

This time, as he swung up, he kicked this old pony in the belly as hard as he could and rode off, not a buck in him, just plain good horse. You could spin him on his hind legs and what a stop! He'd turn left or right as smooth as silk. Ted stepped down and the horse trading began. This guy's been around some too. He finally got Ted to give him $175.00 for the horse.

The deal was all made and we loaded the horse in the pickup and headed south for this rancher's place, going down the main road to Missoula. We were driving along when Ted said, "There's Bill right there." Ted turned off onto a dirt road where

a guy was fixing some fence.

Ted said, "I got that saddle horse I was telling you about."

Now, Bill was 73 years old and pretty well used. You could see he was used to hard life and work. This guy looked at the horse in the pickup, then walked around and looked at the other side. You could tell he liked what he was looking at.

He said, "Well, unload him. You don't expect me to ride him in there do you?"

Ted jumped the horse out of the pickup, tightened the cinch and started to climb on him.

Bill said, "No, I'll ride him myself." Like me, Ted was sure this was the wrong way to sell a horse like this one.

Well, the old boy swung up and so did the horse. Both were four feet in the air and doing their best. You could see this wasn't the first time Bill was ever on a bucking horse. He was doing a fine job but the horse won and laid him flat. He sure took out a big homestead in the middle of that road.

Ted ran down the road, caught the horse, kicked him in the belly and swung up and rode back to us, just as good as an old dog. He started to apologize to Bill, but Bill stopped him and said, "How much?"

"Six hundred fifty dollars," Ted said. "He's really a cow horse."

Bill said, "I'll take him."

Ted said, "You don't want him, Bill. You can't ride him."

Bill said, "I know and I ain't going to try. But I've got three young bucks working for me who think they can. This is going to be fun." And he paid Ted on the spot.

As we went down the road to dump the horse at Bill's place, Ted said, "That damn horse near killed me. I sure hit hard, but I'd do 'er again for $475.00 profit."

HELP YOURSELF

It has always been a custom in this country to help out a friend or neighbor. I think this is so in most rural areas.

Anyway, my friend Howie was just leaving for work in Missoula when a Mercedes drove up and out stepped this happy-go-lucky character by the name of Todd. Todd's wife just sat in the car, grinning out the window at Howie. This was along in August and it was 85 degrees or more in the shade, hotter than rice soup right off the stove.

Todd stepped out and said, "I've got something to show you," walked around to the back of the car to threw open the trunk. When he turned the key in the lock, the lid just flew open and crammed in there was 400 pounds of brown bear.

Todd said, "I need somewhere to skin him out. Can I use one of your buildings?"

Howie said, "Don't you realize the bear season isn't even open? Why'd you shoot him?"

"I didn't," said Todd. Some trucker hit him on the highway. I couldn't leave it to rot on the road could I? If I can get him skinned, I can make a nice rug out of his hide."

Howie said, "I've got to go to work. You'll have to skin him yourself. Let's drag him in here — it's the closest building to the car."

Well, they wrestled the bear out of the trunk, which was quite a job as he had started to swell up and was getting quite an odor to him. They drug the bear into the nearby outbuilding.

Howie said, "Help yourself to my hunting knives and I'll see you later. I'm late now for work."

Summer in Copenhaver Country, circa 1947.

Now, I guess Todd made out fine because he was long gone when Howie got home from work and Howie thought no more about the incident. Everything went fine for three or four days but Howie kept smelling something funny and it was getting pretty bad, so he went investigating to see what it was. When he opened the door on the outbuilding, he sure found out. There on the floor was the damned bear and was he ripe! Blow flies and all.

Howie got on the phone and called Todd. "Get up here and take care of this cockeyed bear," he demanded.

It seems that our friend planned to get his pickup and come back that night and dispose of the carcass but, being a wheeler and dealer, he got mixed up with one of those crooked little sticks and a little white ball. Whether he was looking for the ball or broke the stick I don't know, but Mr. Bear plumb slipped his mind.

Now, as I said before, this bear was ripe but when they moved him he sure got riper; wouldn't even stay together in one piece. Todd got sick and Howie was close to it. When they get to the door, Todd was heaving his last three meals. But all things have to come to an end and they finally got everything taken care of, except for a month of airing out the building.

Howie said, "I don't know who caused the worst mess, the bear or Todd."

It was a great lesson proving that you should never say "help yourself" unless you stay and watch.

HONORING A WRITER

We have a preacher who honors us by speaking at our little church quite often. Now this man and his wife are such people that whether in the pulpit or out in the corral they put themselves so deeply under your hide that you feel such a privilege just to call them your friends.

Lynn is a guy who always has a story to tell. Lots of humor. I enjoy hearing him tell of his experiences, especially the one about the young minister who spoke at their church one Sunday. He gave a great sermon with forcefulness and such a great message that they asked him to return the next Sunday. Now they were in need of a pastor for their church, so asked him back a third time. At last they offered him the job.

After each sermon he would wave his right hand in the air, then turn and wave his left hand in the air. One of the church leaders got him in the corner one day and asked him, "I'm just curious, why do you wave your hands after each sermon?"

"Well, it's like this," said the young man. "I just can't write my own sermons, but the Lord gave me the ability of great power in delivery of my sermons. So I find the best sermons I can and memorize them. When I finish, I feel I have to honor the writer so I make the quotation marks by waving my arms at the end of each sermon."

And there was another young preacher who applied for a job at this country church in a rural area. This young man was a very well-met person with personality plus, could hold the congregation's attention and always had a sermon with a great message.

After serving in the pulpit for a few Sundays and visiting church members around the country for a week or so, the elders had a meeting to decide if they would hire him as their permanent pastor. Well, they called a meeting and were split in their decision whether to hire him or not. Some said they didn't think he was sincere in his faith. The chairman said, "We'll call him in and you can ask him about it."

The young man was shocked that anyone would doubt his faith and asked, "Why do you think that?"

The elder said, "Everybody likes you and your delivery is masterful, but you always wear a belt on your pants and a pair of red suspenders also."

"What's the red suspenders got to do with my faith," asked the reverend.

"Well, if you don't have faith that just the suspenders or belt will hold your pants up, where would you be if your faith was really put to the test?"

MY FRIEND, DON'T SAY "TAINT SO"
I TOLD YOU IT'D BE IN MY NEXT BOOK

I got a call from Norm Hansen from over on the Indian side, of the mountains, Flathead that is, somewhere out of Polson along the lake. He said, "Howard, I'm sending four guys and some stock over. Can they pack out of your place and leave the truck there? I'll come and get it. Sure would appreciate it if you gave them a hand getting started on this pack trip. They plan to come out at Holland Lake, where I'll pick them up."

I said, "Sure," and forgot it all. Just too busy I guess.

Well, when these fellows got here I was busy getting ready for another trip. But, remembering my promise to Norm, I said to ole Ted, who worked for me, "Help them get started will you?"

Pretty quick here came Ted and said, "They've got to have another mule. I can't get it all on the stock they brought with them."

I said, "Give them old Hungry and tell them to leave him at Holland Lake. Then we can pick him up when we come out there after this trip. Tell them to tell McCan what the deal is."

Well, three days later as we came to Limestone Creek in the Bob Marshall Wilderness, across the creek waded one of these fellows to stop me. I said, "What can I do for you?"

He said, "We're in trouble. Don't know what's wrong with Norm's mules. Every time we try to saddle them they just kick at us and buck the saddle off before we can fasten the cinch."

I told the boys to go ahead. I'd see what was wrong and catch up. I rode across the creek to their camp and one of the other guys said, "Your mule is the only gentle one in the works."

Now, I knew Norm's mules were gentle. He wouldn't give them stock that was otherwise. I walked up to the closest mule they had tied to a tree. He whirled and kicked up enough to say, "Leave me alone." Looking at his back, I saw a big saddle gald right over the kidneys. The next one had a bad cinch gald. All four mules were sored pretty good. Even their saddle horses had a good start at getting cinch sores.

I said, "Where are your pads?"

When I looked at them I could see why the mules were in trouble. Norm had some deer hair pads, which are good, but you have to clean them because the horse hair and sweat dries in little balls on them. You have to use your curry comb and scrape it off the pads or it will build up in a bump and rub the mule's back raw.

I said, "Where's your curry comb?"

"What's a curry comb?"

I reached in my saddle pocket and brought out mine. I cleaned the pads and washed the cinches in the creek. Norm's stock was soft and fat from no use and on hot days they'd sweat a lot. When turned loose to graze at night, they'd roll in the sand and the sand would stick to their backs. Now, as they walked along, the movement of the saddle blanket acted as a sandpaper, causing raw spots. I showed the fellows how to wash these sores with warm salt water, and rode off and left them.

As I got on my horse to go, one of them came up with a curry comb in his hand and said, "When we left, Norm told me to stick this in my saddle pocket but I didn't know what it was for."

When we got to Holland Lake ten days later, old Hungry was munching hay in the corral so I guess they made it out okay.

TRICKS OF THE TRADE
OR TED TRADES

One of the oldest professions on earth is that of a trader. Call it what you want — barter, swapping, horse trading, dealing or just plain beating the other guy at his own deal — I love it and the stories that go with it.

My dear mother used to say there never was an honest trader. They were always looking for some way to beat someone else. Well, that's the name of the game. You only trade to better yourself, never even, because if you can't better yourself there's no use of trading.

One thing I learned long ago — never trade unless you get some boot. What I mean by boot is your pocket knife for Joe's knife, but make Joe give you two-bits extra because yours is shinier than his. Then, at least, you gain two things for one. If both knives are of the same value you've gained two-bits on the side.

There's been fortunes made and lost this way. So to me trading is a "You beat me or I'll beat you" deal with lots of challenge. You'd better have your eyes open because the other guy is only going to tell you what he wants you to know and, if he can trade you a hat with a hole in it for a new one, he's going to do it. Don't forget the boot.

Say, did you ever play marbles when you were a kid? Well that's where I got my first education on this trading bit. Every kid on the street in Great Falls, Montana, had his pockets bulging with marbles. All you needed for a game was another kid. The strips of lawn on each side of the sidewalk had bare circles where the grass

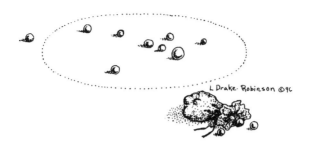

L. Drake-Robinson ©96

never grew because of kids, around a circle, playing marbles. The guys watering and mowing the grass spent most of their time chasing kids away from our special spots — which were smooth. The grass didn't have a chance.

I've tried to remember the names of these marbles. I know we had Pattys made of clay, brown with 2 black spots on them. Ten of them worth an Emery (colored glass) and five Emeries worth one larger one. Mebby a Flint. Then 10 to 20 Flints equalled an Agate, depending on coloration and size. Also, a Steeley made of polished steel and so on. Agates cost a lot of money at that time, from 15 cents up to 75 cents for big ones.

Well, there were two kids who won all of the marble tournaments at this time. One was a preacher's son named Totson, whose right hand pocket always bulged with Agates of all sizes. How I envied him. He was rich!

One day I found an Agate laying in the grass by one of these circles. Was I happy! It was clear on the bottom with a dark ridge across the middle and red (trees) along the top. It was a beautiful Montana Agate. I used it for my shooter in special games.

Now this Totson kid really admired my Agate shooter and one day he said, "Tell you what I'll do," as he stuck his hand into his Agate pocket. I'll just feel and grab one Agate, pull my hand out and trade you for that shooter of yours."

Now I could just see him opening his hand and there would

be one of those 75 cent Aggies.

I said, "It's a deal."

Out came his hand and he dumped it into mine. There was a marble in it, but it was a great big Patty with chips out of it till it couldn't roll on the cement sidewalk. I'd just said it was a deal, so now he had my Agate shooter and I had my big old Patty and a lesson in horse trading.

As I grew older, I began listening to the men talk about horse trades, always a great topic at that time. They'd tell of how badly they'd beaten some guy and how some other guy had taken them for a good ride. Horse trading was always a great maker of conversation at the bar, dinner table or around the campfire, with lots of humor and laughter — much needed virtues in the 1920's and 30's.

One of the oldest in the book of "honest horse trades" was what I call the white glove treatment. If you were sharp, you'd notice a guy with his saddle horse right at the head of the line at the sale gate to the ring. He'd have on a pair of buckskin gloves, petting his horse on the nose, rubbing him very gently. When his turn came to ride through the ring, he'd swing up and ride in just as nice as you pleased. He'd turn his horse this way and that, back him up a couple of times, step off and jerk his saddle off and show the crowd what a nice back the horse had. Then he'd turn him loose in the ring, pick up his gear and walk out. The horse would sell fast. No fuss, not scared of the crowd — just nice.

When the poor buyer got his horse home and went to ride him, well, it was a different ball game. This old pony was just as liable as not to stick its head in the sand and dump the proud owner in the corner of the corral.

You see, if you caught this white-gloved cowboy and looked at those pretty gloves, you'd find the palms of each glove was punched full of little round holes. Mebby, at first, you'd think he cut these holes to keep his hands cool. But I don't think so. Take a good smell of them. This old boy would take a pad of cotton or gauze, soak it with chloroform, and then rub it across the horse's nose until his eyes looked glassy and shiny, sort of sleepy-like. (If you did it too much he'd go to sleep and fall down.)

These old boys knew when to stop. At the right time, you could step up on the horse and it would do whatever you wanted. Just don't do it too fast or too long or you were in trouble. So the buyer thinks the horse is gentle all the time — he's not even half green broke. And the buyer was then stuck with a green horse.

You can do the same with a horse that always wants to buck. Give him a few snorts and you can ride him till he comes to.

I knew one man, who used to be in the Ovando area when I was a kid, that would go to fairs and rodeos around the country and advertise: "I'll bet $50 to anyone who brings me a horse I can't ride without him bucking. But the horse must be halter broke to lead."

I'll call this man Mat. He'd rub these yeller gloves all over the horse's face and nose, all the time telling the horse how nice he was. When the time was right, Mat would grab a handful of mane and swing up on the horse bareback and ride him around a circle a couple of times, step off and collect his $50. He knew his business, and I never heard of him paying many bets off. He just collected them.

Here's a modern day version of the same thing only a different color. This all came about due to World War II and new developments in the field of medical tranquilizers. When I came home after World War II, I needed horses and mules. I'd go to the sales, but there just weren't many local horses. Too many had been shipped to France during the war both for food and Army use, so the sale rings began to fill with stock from Canada, Washington, Wyoming and even as far away as Kansas and Missouri. I'd take the truck to a sale and load up with 10 head of saddle horses, bring them home and dump them in the corral. The next morning the boys and I would go out to ride them and see how good a bunch of dude horses I'd gotten.

We'd saddle them up and start riding them. Some you couldn't saddle without tying up a hind foot. They weren't even green broke but had handled through the ring real well the day

L. Drake - Robinson © 96

before. Well, these old boys had learned the act of using a needle and tranquilizer. It works. If you learn just how much to shoot the horses with, you can pick up their feet and shoe them without any trouble — or ride them just like a gentle horse, but not for very long. One time, out of a load of 10 head, I ended up with only four horses that I could use. So, I took the others back and sold them at the next sale for canners.

Another good deal, which didn't last long, was to sit at a sale and watch for a good, gentle horse someone would ride through that looked good but appeared to be ill kept, with long, scraggly mane, dirty, long hair on the fetlocks making his feet look clumsy and big. To top it off, the horse's tail would be dragging the ground and was full of straw and dirt. The bid would usually be canner price, very low.

We'd bid him in and then take him out behind the corral and trim his mane and tail, boot him (cut all the long hair from his ankles) and wash him with a garden hose. We'd dry him down and then ride him back through the ring, and sell him again.

I've had the original owner come up and say, "Was that my horse you just sold?"

We'd say, "Yes. Would you buy a dirty hat?"

Sometimes we'd double our money on the same horse, but even if we couldn't do that we always made a few bucks. Finally the sale owner stopped us. He made it a rule that no animal could be resold through his ring on the same day. Now I ask you, wasn't that interfering with private enterprise?

Another trick was if you had a dead-headed horse that showed no life or spirit, just a plug, you'd ride him down a horse or two from the sale gate, waiting your turn to go in. You'd have a rag soaked with turpentine in your hand. Just before your time, you'd step off and rub this wet rag under the plug's tail, wetting the hair and skin good. Then you'd step back on him and by the time the horse in front of you was sold, the turpentine would start to burn or sting your horse. Up would come his tail in a nice arch, and his ears and head would perk up.

I'm telling you he'd snap his feet up mighty pretty. You could show him with a tight rein real nice. It didn't hurt him at all, but in 30 minutes the turpentine had died and you had the same old dead-headed plug, but he was owned by someone else and you'd bettered yourself a bunch with money.

SHOOT'N ED

In booking hunters over the years it has always been a problem of how to answer questions asked by prospective hunters. One often asked is, "Can I shoot off your saddle horses?" My answer is, "No, I've never seen a man that can shoot elk from the top of a horse."

One day I had to swallow all of this. I came down off the mountain from hunting Hellgate Canyon on Rapid Creek. Me and my hunter had just got to where we'd left our horses that morning, tied off the Rapid Creek trail. We were mounted and ready to head for camp eight miles away when around the bend came Ed Geary, with two hunters behind him. Ed was an old outfitter and we camped close together in the Danaher Valley.

He hollered at me, "How's hunting?"

I said, "If I can just get this guy an elk we'll be full for this trip, but today's our last day. We pull out tomorrow. Had a chance today but we messed up, let them get our wind. How you doing?"

He said, "If me and these two boys can get a couple I'd be full too, but it don't look good. Seems like the elk have all crawled in a hole and pulled it in after them."

He was headed for camp, too, so me and my guest fell in behind him and headed down the trail. We hadn't gone far when we came to a long park in the timber sloping off below to Rapid Creek. Just as we rode out in the open, out of the creek came an old cow with about 30 head of elk right behind her — all headed up the side of the mountain to Sugar Loaf. Like a flash, Old Ed

left that old black horse he was riding, with his rifle in his hands. I'll swear that before his feet hit the ground that gun was barking. I don't remember for sure, but I think he shot six times. Now, these elk were running up the side of a mountain at 150 to 200 yards away.

Ed threw his hat in the air and yelled, "Get your licenses out. There's your damn elk and one for me."

I couldn't believe it, but there laying on the hillside were four dead elk and nearby were three very pleased hunters. That late in the season they didn't care who did the shooting; they wanted meat and I'm sure they built their own story of the kill before they got home. And I could never say again that no man can ride a horse and shoot elk.

Shoot'n Ed Geary.

Now old Ed has gone on to hunt a new country. He's no longer with us; he paid his dues and left us here to fight politics and taxes. He was a great Irishman and is missed more than he ever dreamed.

I feel I can tell this other story about him because his son told it in his honor at a memorial we had for Ed in the school gym. In attendance were, from wall to wall in that gymnasium, people from far and near.

Ed had a vocabulary that only a teamster late for dinner should have. He never realized his cussing when he talked and no one ever took offense at it. As he talked, it just rolled out so easy and smooth. His language was as rough and rugged as he was.

Now Ed had two children. One was a boy. They were at the dinner table one day when the son asked for some G-- d--- spuds. Old Ed came alive and grabbed him by the neck and out the door they went, where Ed patted his fanny and said, "Who do you think you are? Nobody, but nobody, talks that way at my table."

The kid said, "But Dad, you say that all the time."

Ed said, "Not at my table I don't and neither do you."

Now, Ed's wife got a tape recorder and taped a few meals. Then one day when all were eating, she turned it on. Ed slammed down his knife and fork and said, "Who the hell is that talking that way?"

Ellen said, "That's you, honey."

"No it ain't," said Ed, though it cleaned up his vocabulary for awhile — the lesson was soon forgotten.

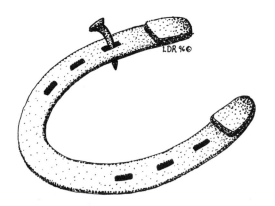

HORSE DOCTORS
— NOT REALLY A VET —

When you make your living for three-fourths of a century with horses and mules and a few cows and dogs, you soon learn to listen to all the home remedies you hear. It just doesn't happen that none of them get sick.

You learn how to drench them, give them an enema, midwife foals, even how to perform a Caesarean birth. Yes, I've done that, too, following directions from a sick horse doctor who couldn't make it. The cow and calf made it! Hurray for me. You learn to use a needle for sleeping sickness and what antibiotics work best on mules or horses.

I'll never forget one episode of sleeping sickness. I had 120 head of horses and mules to doctor. Vet price — $11.00 per head. No outfitter has that kind of money to waste in the spring. So what do you do? You buy the syringe and medicine and start laying those old ponies on their sides and learning how it's done. A few days later, with six ribs broken off my backbone, a few stitches in the back of my head, 29 stitches in Howie's head, a trip to the hospital and the following month a sizeable bill from those people who patched us up, we'd got the job done for $3.00 per head and only lost three horses. The medicine must not have worked because we sure did.

Then this guy came along one fall and said, "Say, Howard, I've got one section of good horse pasture I'll give you a great deal on. I planted it to intermediate wheat grass and it's been too wet. I can't combine it for seed."

I said, "What's intermediate wheat grass?"

He said, "It's a new grass they've come up with and the price on the seed beats grain all to pieces. But it's been so wet it won't ripen."

I said, "I'll go look at it. Will horses eat it?"

Jim said, "You bet."

Well it sure was pretty grass and thick and tall. Now his price was sure right — $5.00 per head per month. I liked that, so when packing season was over we turned 115 head of horses and mules into this pasture of grass, just as happy as if we had good sense.

I went over to see how they were doing, and to drop salt for them, about three weeks later. What a mess! We had six dead horses and there were many sick horses down and some were hobbling around, all humped up. One look and I knew they sure was bound up. They were constipated, plugged solid.

There was only one thing to do — tube them with mineral oil and epsom salts. To accomplish this, you run a tube up a nostril and down into their stomach. Then you pump warm mineral oil and epsom salts into their stomachs. If this doesn't work, you try from the other end. Well we saved all of them but 11 of those animals, the biggest loss I ever had with stock. It seems that the glucose in the joints of the straw cause compacted bowels unless the animals also intake abundant water.

WHAT'S WRONG

What has happened to the hunter? As I sit here and look back over the past 65 years as a hunter, outfitter and guide, I become scared. I go back to 1930 because I can remember best and am old enough to realize what all this means. Some people call it progress or say it's because there are more people. I say numbers have nothing to do with it and progress is questionable. My theory is the new formula of values that we have today and I am deeply concerned about it.

The 1994 hunting season really brought this to a point of disgust and concern with me. It was seldom that year that I saw a game warden's pickup that didn't have a couple of confiscated elk or deer in it. Most of these were animals someone had shot and left lay in the woods or by the roadside, all illegally shot.

Years ago people shot elk and deer out of season, I know, but they hauled them home and ate them. Illegal, yes, but the people did not shoot, kill and let go to waste on the hill. It was seldom I talked to a hunter this past season who had not found an elk or deer someone had shot and left lay. In the small length of time I was in the field I came upon six different elk that had been shot, with snow on the ground and a distinct blood trail. In no case was there a hunter track following the blood trail from where the elk was first shot.

Then on the Monture Game Range below Ovando, there were 100 to 150 elk feeding among as many cattle just off Highway 200. A number of cars and pickups stopped and the occupants jumped out, and then began shooting at the elk. No cattle were hit, but two or three illegal elk lay dead, plus three more cow elk found later in the day that had to be killed. Was that all that was hit? I rather think not, for the elk ran up over the hill out of sight.

Another example I came across was three elk laying dead just below a road on a grassy hillside, one cow dressed out, two more laying dead in the sagebrush. Farther down the hill were two more wounded that had to be killed.

Another one is the incident of finding a nice mature bull laying in an accessible spot, not dressed out, with just his cape and antlers gone.

Recently, a pickup went by my house with deer feet sticking up over the box. That's not unusual. But 30 minutes later a neighbor stopped, mad as a wet hen. He told me a guy in a pickup had just thrown a deer into the garbage dumpster. I drove

A good part of Copenhaver Country for Howard for many, many years was to lead a string of pack animals through the wilderness. Here he's shown fording the North Fork of the Blackfoot River sometime in the early 1950s.

out to see for myself. Sure enough, there was a beautiful buck deer in the dump. No head!

How many such animals were found in the area of Monture and Ovando Mountain I do not know, but undoubtedly there were more that no one found. The ones I speak of were in very accessible, open country, lightly forested, and the situation doesn't make sense. I can't recall a year as bad as this one.

After the season, why would two grown men, driving down the road in the middle of winter and, upon seeing a bull elk feeding on an open hillside, stop their car, jump out and shoot it, and then get back in their car and simply drive away? Luckily, they were seen, reported and were subsequently arrested and convicted.

Another incident reported in our area involved unknown people in a car travelling along the highway who, upon seeing some elk eating hay with some horses in a field adjacent to the highway, stopped and shot at the elk. They missed both elk and horses, and buildings, but drove off before the rancher on whose land the elk and horses were feeding could get to them.

The game wardens work their heads off. The sportsmen shell out thousands of dollars to support game, donating to organizations such as the Rocky Mountain Elk Foundation to provide habitat for the game, pay for licenses to be able to hunt, support ways of gaining access, winter range, transplanting — and ranchers donate acres of grass and access. This is big money for Montana and something needs to be done to protect it. Just to let a few destroy it hurts us all.

Sure, we were getting too many cow elk on concentrated areas due to closed hunting areas and mebby not enough cow-only permits in our area. Then the game department came along with the A-7 tag, which gives the hunter the right to harvest a cow elk. It surely looked good to me. Areas that were not hunted could now be used where the elk concentration was.

Then this little word "but" comes along. A-7 tags were definitely a management tool that should work, but in the hands of inexperienced hunters, and first-time hunters, it can't. When you

This is part of the great hunting country where Howard and his brothers, including Gene (pictured), hunted elk over the years. This is the famed Danaher Basin in the Bob Marshall Wilderness.

put tools in the hands of someone who doesn't realize how to use them the tool becomes useless.

With elk that are used to running in large groups in a more or less protected area, the elk, when disturbed, will mill and wait for the lead cow to show them what to do. Road hunters, upon seeing a large group of elk along a road, stop and shoot. Just at elk. If none fall on the spot, they look for another bunch! Never checking for a blood trail?

And don't tell me "No, that doesn't happen." I've seen it happen right off Highway 200 east of Ovando. A few days after the previous incident involving the horses and the elk, three cow elk were found not a mile from the spot where that shooting took place. One guy got a five point bull on the spot. Not another hunter went to see if they'd hit a thing.

My answer to this is a whole paragraph of question marks.

My friends, something has to change or we will lose our hunting heritage, our right to this kind of life and our game. STOP AND THINK!!! I've been an outfitter and guide and hunted for three-fourths of a century. I have found you have to teach people to shoot at a spot on an animal, not just at the animal. Never take your eyes off of the animal till it's down. Be sure there is not another one behind the one you're shooting at. Rifles today will shoot through one elk and wound another. Never flock shoot, something I see happening a lot today. The hunter needs to know what he is doing.

There is a growing disrespect for the value of our wildlife. This is a precious resource. AGAIN, STOP AND THINK!!!

MIKE AND THE MULES

When you hear a story told that you really enjoy, you can stop and think and you'll connect it to some actual happening someplace along the line. Well, Reverend Hodges and wife had lunch with us the other day and told this story his father loved to tell him when he was a boy.

Now, it seems this preacher owned a pair of mules. He had trained and broke them to drive his own way. They reacted to his every command, finally becoming the top pulling team at all the fairs in North Dakota — winning all prize events.

Finally, there came a time when he had to sell the pair. A neighbor bought them and the preacher explained how he had trained them so well and how you should drive them. He said he had trained them to voice command only. Here's the advice he gave: When you want them to go you should say, "Praise the Lord." Never say "Giddy up." When you want them to stop you say, "Amen." They don't know what "Whoa" means, and never pull on the reins.

The neighbor said, "Fine," and hooked them to his buckboard, jumped on the seat and hollered, "Praise the Lord." Away went the mules across the prairie, getting faster all the time. Mr. John Farmer was pulling on the reins, hollering, "Whoa!" at the top of his voice.

Suddenly, the instructions he'd been given came back to him and he hollered, "Amen." Those mules slid to a dead stop so sudden it threw the driver over the dash and down onto the wagon tongue. He fought to get back up on the seat, all the while looking at the river down below. Finally he made it back up to the seat and, with a sigh of relief, loudly exclaimed, "Praise the Lord." Like a flash those hardtails ran over the bank and into the river — farmer, buckboard, mules and all.

Now, this brought to mind what happened to Mike, a friend of mine. All my life I've studied people and, most of the rest has been spent counselling horses and mules.

Now horses are something you can understand but a mule — that's another thing. One thing for sure, I have learned you have to get a mule to do what you want done by having him do it the way he wants to do it. Then your problems are over.

Mike is a great guy, a photographer working for the *Missoulian* newspaper in Missoula, Montana. He does a lot of special assignment work and, well, I was posing for him on an assignment and he was telling me some of his experiences. This one sure fits the bill.

I know mules and I can just see those old ears turning back and forward — a sign that their minds are working.

It seems there was to be a celebration of some kind in Missoula and the paper wanted to advertise it. So, poor Mike was chosen to get pictures and a story for them. He was to take a drive to a ranch where they were driving some mules on a covered wagon to be used in the parade. They needed some good action pictures for the paper.

When Mike arrived at the ranch, the mules were hitched to the wagon, just as quiet as if they had good sense. A teamster was tying a canvas down on the rear of the wagon when Mike drove up and parked his shiny Honda right in the middle of the yard. Then he started arranging his camera, film, etc.

Now it had been a dismal and rainy morning, so Mike was afraid the pictures wouldn't be good. But just as he stepped out of the car, the clouds broke away and out came the sun, bright and clear. Mike looked up and exclaimed, "Praise the Lord."

Like a flash those long eared Democrats hooked to the wagon said, "What are we waiting for?" Away they went, around the barn. One of the teamsters has one arm tangled in the rope and

L. Drake-Robinson © 96

canvas; now, he was dragging behind the wagon.

Mike grabbed his camera and said, "Now I'll get some real action pictures — on the spot news."

He no more than got his camera ready when around the house came the mules, wagon and some ill-gotten fence, with the teamster still dragging behind — all headed for Mike and his Honda.

Mike said, at first, "They won't run over my car." Then he screamed, "Yes they will!" He threw himself on the floorboards.

Right up over the hood came those long ears with wagon still in tow. These hardtails were losing no time, almost as if they were enjoying their one-sided race. When the front axle of the wagon hit the support of the windshield, the wagon tongue broke and away went the mules in a cloud of dust.

The wagon stopped right on top of Mike's car, rocked back and forth, and then tipped over — with wagon, car and Mike all in one pile. What a mess! When things settled down and a few Band-Aids had been applied to Mike, he found himself the owner of a different car. The Honda was a total wreck.

Now, Mike is a quiet spoken guy and never told us what he called those mules. (Mebby he just forgot to say, "Amen.")

LEAVING NO TRACE

Before I can say much about "Leaving No Trace" in the wilderness, I want to give you an idea of where I am coming from to be able to form any opinion.

My idols as a small boy were "Old Kid Young," Joe Stattler, Smokie Deneau, and also Tom Danaher along with the Praust boys, all of whose names are embedded in the Bob Marshall Wilderness and Scapegoat Wilderness areas. Young's Creek, Stattler Creek, Danaher Valley, Smoke's Bridge on the Northfork and Sullivan Cabin on Hawn Creek where Smokie and Rose Bushbalm lived during World War I, are all named after these old-timers.

Then in the 1920's, when I was old enough, I followed in their tracks. Back then you just went your merry way fishing, hunting, trapping or whatever. You never thought of what it would be like in 1994. You felt you owned this big, beautiful country and never gave a thought that it may not be here forever. Everyone was at fault for thinking that way; the Forest Service, outfitters, Fish and Game and private users never realized what was going on.

I have read transcripts written by fathers of wilderness thinking — Aldo Leopold, Bob Marshall, Teddy Roosevelt, Olas Murie, and personally knew a couple of these men. One of the things that sticks in my mind is what one of these boys said — we cannot build wilderness. We can only protect what is left to the best of our ability.

Another pamphlet I read was written, I believe, by

Leopold, "What Worth the Wilderness." This made me wake up and change my attitude about using wilderness.

If you have ever read Teddy Roosevelt's *"Diary of Hunting the Yellowstone,"* you know that he thought he was a great sportsman. Early in his career, he shot as many as five bull elk in one day, leaving them to the bears, coyotes and birds — these are his own words — taking only the best trophy heads. His attitude changed and he became the greatest protector of our game and a father of wilderness. He spoke of travelling for 14 hours on foot and at night he could still see the smoke of their previous night's fire — no thought of making sure the campfire was dead out.

Do you see what I mean? We had the same attitude and abused this country without realizing it for many years. We threw our cans in the brush or buried them along streams in soft ground, built fires anywhere, and rode down the trail leaving Mother Nature to clean up the mess. She couldn't. Now she cries for help.

Howard and a friend take a moment to savor the awesome mountain ruggedness of the Bob Marshall Wilderness.

Do you see what I mean about changing our attitude? What brought this so deeply to my mind was the beautiful wild islands I saw laid to destruction during World War II in the South Pacific Islands. It bothered me and I thought a great deal about it. Then, in 1949, at an outfitter and Forest Service meeting I hit them with a plan. Simply put, everybody packing into the wilderness areas would pack out what they packed in. You should have heard the reception I got. The supervisor of Region One hit the ceiling. "Do you mean to say you want us to pack all garbage out from all our ranger stations?" he said.

I said, "Yes."

He said, "You're crazy."

I finally got three other outfitters to agree with me to start doing this very thing. Herb Toelke, Tom Edwards, and Dick Hickey of Lairds Lodge all pitched in. We even dug out old garbage holes and packed them out. The Forest Service saw it was good and established a "Pack out what you pack in" policy. It has done great things, in my opinion.

About 1953 I was camped at the Young's Creek ford with a big wilderness group. At that time there was a meeting of the heads of each forest district at the Big Prairie Ranger Station. They all came up to my camp for drinks and supper that night with the wilderness group. Some of my guests were perplexed because I had camped them in such a much-used campsite. They felt they deserved a fresh camp all of their own. I talked a number of them into coming along with the group from the Forest Service to take a walk down the river bank for three-fourths of a mile and count how many fire scars and tin cans we could see where other people had camped. We counted 31 different spots that had been scarred up over a number of years.

My question to them: was it better to have a few bigger scarred up camps that can be cleaned up, or a lot of them over the length of the river? I still don't have the answer.

Now, as to "Leaving No Trace." This is hard to do but I believe that distribution of visitors is a big part of the answer. This can be done by opening trails that have been closed for years, and giving out more information on where to get away from the river bottoms to find more enjoyable places of solitude and spectacular scenery.

Equipment is a major factor in back country comfort and efficiency. I believe a stove is a must or you have a fire ring and mussed up area where you try to hide the fire scar. We have tent frames of only a few pounds that save cutting poles to pitch camp. When you're gone, so are the poles.

Livestock is a big factor. When you make camp, either turn them loose to graze, or hobble or picket them away from camp area. Horses that are free to graze do far less damage than those that are picketed. If you are afraid of losing your stock, take them to where the feed is good. In two hours a horse can pretty well fill up. Watch them. If grain or pellets are used, use a feed bag. Don't let them paw where you feed on the ground.

Now we can make all the regulations, rules, etc., we want — but it will be only a bandaid on a big wound.

In the last 10 to 15 years, wilderness use has doubled and mebby tripled. With a projected growth of another 600,000 people in the next five years for western Montana, we are in trouble if we don't prepare for them. These people are not paying these high land prices for only a place to live; they all want to be close to the wilderness areas. My friends, they are going to use them.

In my opinion, from back country experience, we must meet this head-on. Wilderness use must be managed much like the parks, with designated camp areas maintained by Forest Service employees, and trails opened to disperse people from the valley floors. I can even see numbers having to be controlled.

People with livestock must be educated about how, when and where livestock is to be used and taken care of. Many of these people coming to the wilderness will have four or five horses that they have ridden only on private property or bridle pathways. They will have no idea about either their care and handling in the mountains.

I have friends who outfit in the California wilderness and also the far East Coast. What they tell me scares me to death about

A packstring under the overwhelming grandeur of the famed Chinese Wall in the Bob Marshall Wilderness, a part of "Copenhaver Country" for the past 80 years.

our great "Bob." The Bob Marshall Wilderness is so accessible from all sides and, in reality, it is gentle country compared to other wild areas. Education is the answer.

If you have people, you have traces. Ten people will make more traces in one day than 10 head of horses and mules in a week. Stock spreads out. People stick together, in a bunch.

I hate to see it come but I'm afraid that so many regulations are in store for the Bob and Scapegoat Wilderness that a trip to Sugar Loaf Mountain or Pentagon will be no enjoyment at all. A lot of regulations have been put on the outfitters, trying to "Leave no trace" — lightweight equipment, cutting stock, cutting numbers in parties, cutting use days, restricting outfitters to certain areas. It hasn't worked because the restrictions aren't aimed at the cause of the problem. From what I have seen in the last few years, there are more private livestock in the Bob and Scapegoat areas than all the outfitters together own. So, in my opinion, much of the new

"Leave no trace" has to come from the private sector. Outfitters have to protect wilderness to protect their business.

I wish I could solve just one of these problems, but I can't. But we can try.

TODD AND CHRISS

I've written about guiding Sarah, my granddaughter, on elk and deer hunts. She's in college now so I'm hunting down line on grandkids now. I've got a lot of hunting to do if I guide all of them — probably be at least 109 years by the time they've all reached that hunting age.

This past fall Todd, Steve's boy, was here so we decided to take a day's hunt up Monture and try for a good buck deer. The next morning it is snowing big, heavy, wet flakes, almost rain, and there was about six inches of wet snow on the ground. We left before daylight and drove about 12 miles to where I expected to hunt. It was still too dark to shoot when we got there, so we sat in the pickup, drinking coffee, waiting for daylight.

Todd has already shot his first bull elk and a muley buck the season before. He had ridden into Steve's (his dad's) hunting camp and the next day Steve took him down on the bench. They had not gone far when a bull bugled off to the south of them. Steve bugled back at him, putting all the fight and romance he could into that call. Back came the response from the bull, a bugle that was loud, clear and ready to go. Todd and his dad squatted under a tree and watched; they could hear the bull coming, thrashing limbs off trees and grunting.

All of a sudden, there he stood, right out in the open about 150 yards up the ridge.

"Hold low and let him have it," whispered Steve.

Todd laid that old 25-35 on him and when it boomed the bull hit the ground. Didn't even kick.

Todd exclaimed, "I didn't know a gun would kill them that fast!"

Steve told him, "This is a good lesson for you. A gun will kill another hunter just as quick. Always know for sure what you're shooting at."

Later that year, between hunts, Steve had a spare afternoon so he and Todd drove up an old logging road near Ovando, on Elk Mountain, looking for a muley buck. They hunted all afternoon, saw some deer off so far they couldn't get to them and one time there were other hunters between them and the game. So they went back to the pickup; it was late anyhow. But as they drove down the mountain Todd says, "There's one!" Steve stopped and Todd jumped out, rested his rifle over the hood and "bang," he had his muley buck. They dressed it out, drug it down the hill and slid it into the pickup. Then they stopped at my place to show me his muley.

Todd said, "Boy, it's sure easy."

I said, "You wait till next year."

But he's got a five-point bull and a nice muley to brag about. And he's been told all the "what to do" and "do nots" of hunting for 14 years: Always shoot at a spot on your game. Never take your eyes or gun off the animal till you now it's down for good. Never rush after wounded game. Go to the track, look for blood; then sit down and give them 15 minutes. I know that's a long time to sit when you're a young (or old) hunter, but it's a must. Then follow your game tracks slow, one step at a time, looking everywhere for a movement or an ear, eye or some off-colored spot in the vegetation.

Well, Todd and I sat there waiting for daylight. Several rigs with hunters passed us and finally one turned up this road where we planned to hunt.

I said, "We might as well look for a new spot. They'll just spook all the game, driving up there ahead of us." We'd planned to hike up that road a ways and hunt down.

So, we drove on over to Shanley Creek and by the time we got there, it was just getting to be daylight. We drove along slowly to just past Cottonwood Lake turn-off, which is on sort of a flat with heavy brush and timber up this steep mountainside. Sloppy wet snow was hanging on all the brush and fir trees — a regular soaker of a jungle. The woods were really wet, with a drizzle of warm rain coming down. And if you've ever walked through a mess like this, you know what's going to happen.

We were poking along in the pickup, looking for fresh tracks, when Todd hollered, "There's one! He's huge!" I stopped. Out the door flew Todd and run down the road. He stopped and I saw him throw up his gun, shoot up the ridge above him. "I got him," he yelled, and was gone after that buck like a greyhound on a fresh rabbit. I yelled and hollered for him to go slow but he paid ho heed.

I didn't hear him shoot again so I got out and climbed up the mountain to where the deer had been standing when he first shot at it. Sure enough, there is plenty of blood on both sides of the tracks, meaning it was hit hard. But I'm soaking wet by then and my game leg says, "You've gone far enough, old man." It was slick and Todd's tracks were about 12 feet apart, and since I only step three feet at a time on level going, I just sat down and listened. Finally, I heard a shot.

I decided there was no need for me to follow his tracks all over the side of the hill when there was hot coffee in the pickup. Besides, I'd let this kid learn a few things about hunting the hard way. When he came back, we could then go straight to the deer and not wander all over the sidehill on wet tracks.

But time passes and I'd become pretty well dried out, and out of coffee, just hoping that Todd would show up pretty soon. I heard the sounds of three or four shots, but they were too far off to be Todd doing the shooting; besides, they came from different directions. But I had a good view of the hill from where we were parked; I could look down the road and along the hill about a half mile — all of a sudden here came this guy into view. He was walking along, but you'd almost have to set up two stakes to determine if he was moving.

It was Todd and he was stripped to his undershirt from the waist up, and was covered with blood. I drove down to meet him. He crawled into the pickup and I said, "How many times have you been told never to run after wounded game?"

He said, "Yeah, yeah, I know. But now I *really* know. I got him down here across the creek, right along the road, but he just wouldn't lay down. Shot him four times. He's a big five pointer."

I said, "Todd, if every time you stopped somebody kicked you in the butt, would you stay put?"

We got the buck loaded and went home, planning to get something to eat and then go over on Pearson Creek, across the river, and look for a buck for me while there was still fresh snow.

But when we got home Todd laid down on the floor in the front room while Marg was making us a sandwich. When his folks stopped to pick him up that evening, about 9 o'clock, Todd was still asleep on the floor. But, there also was a nice five-point whitetail hanging in my shop.

While I'm telling tales about people who are not here to defend themselves I might as well tell about Chriss, another of my grandsons. This story involves Chriss' first hunting license and his big chance to get an elk as he drew a cow tag and could shoot either a cow or bull.

Chriss was just 13 years old, slightly over 4'6" tall and a basketball stealing fireball, though he couldn't even see over a good huckleberry bush. Seems like John and Susie don't produce any long-legged kids.

Anyway, I got this telephone call. "Grampa, you want to go hunting with me? Not, "Grampa, will you take me hunting?" But that's alright. I said, "I'll give you a call when I think it looks good. The weather I mean." Before we went on a hunt, I planned to do a little scouting for tracks; it was early in the season yet and I was hoping for some snow.

Well, we got some snow but it ended up with a rain and then a freeze. That snow was just like corn flakes. You'd step on it and it would almost hold you; then it would crunch and you'd break through it. It was just about as noisy as it could get, plus it was very cold in the mornings.

A bull elk responds to a call in a dense stand of lodgepole pine and comes warily in to encounter the source of the call. This sort of hunting experience characterizes the lore of the wilderness that Howard has written about over the years.

Then came a morning it wasn't so cold, so I called Chriss on the phone and says, "I'll pick you up about 6:30 tomorrow morning and we'll see if I can show you an elk. The next morning when I stopped at Chriss' house, my son-law, Chriss's dad, John, came out to the pickup. He made me promise that if we got something that I wouldn't try to drag it out by myself. He said, "You come to the log yard and me and Al will go get it for you. "

He thought I was going to overtax myself, but I thought that he didn't know me very well. My ears ain't long enough to drag or pack an elk out by myself without a mule.

Chriss and I took off, drove down to Dry Gulch, parked the pickup and started up the ridge. I saw right away that this old 80-year-old man wasn't any match for this 13-year-old when it came to going uphill, as I was always behind him.

"Take it slower, Chriss. You'll spook all the game. You've got to watch where you step. Kind of slide your foot under the crust. Don't just stomp it down and break the crust. As you top the ridge don't go straight over. Come up behind a tree or bush and ease around so you can see the other side. If you go over the top you'll be silhouetted against the sky and all game watches all the high spots. Go slow," I said.

Now all of this was not just schooling for Chriss. It was helping an old man save face due to years and steep hills. Chriss, knowing the truth, did his best to follow instructions but he wanted to cover ground and get some shooting done. Well, we hunted up over the top and across this flat country. There were lots of tracks but they make poor soup. Finally, as we were headed back along this steep sidehill, I saw this ole whitetail buck laying in his bed, down the hill a bit. I pointed and whispered to Chriss, "There's your buck."

Like a shot, that buck jumped up and sped down the hill. I never even saw his feet hit the ground. And Chriss bobbed this way and that, trying to get the buck in his sights, but with no luck. It was an impossible shot.

When we got down to the pickup, both Chriss and I were cold so we headed for Grandma's and some hot chocolate and coffee. After we'd finished our warm beverages and a sandwich, and were warmed up, I said, "I'd better take you home."

Now, the night before I'd kept waking up, seeing a bunch of elk looking at me. I often experience this same thing in a kind of fogged mind or dream and usually I'll get game that next day. As we drove up the road to Chriss' I kept thinking about the dream. But I couldn't remember where I'd been in those dreams. When we came to a crossroad, I said to Chriss, "You don't want to go home yet. Let's drive up along the flat and I'll see if I can rattle you up a buck. There are some does and bucks up along the Mail Box Hill. Tell you what I'm going to do. I'm going to leave my knife and gun in the truck and take my deer horns to rattle with. Now she's all up to you. I'll call and you shoot. You got a knife?"

He said, "I got two of them."

We left the pickup, crawled through the fence and were about 100 yards up the side of a draw filled with a dense fir thicket. As we pussyfooted along, I thought I heard something off to our right, down in this thick draw.

"Chriss, you hear anything?" I whispered.

"Right over there." He pointed across the draw. I heard footsteps.

I stood and just listened. Sure enough, Chriss was right. From the loudness of them, I knew it had to be elk. Didn't sound like a light animal.

Whispering to Chriss, I said, "When you see them, don't look at all of them. Look at just one. Hold low and shoot. When we go past that tree, there are going to be a bunch of elk looking right at us. Shoot the first one you get in your scope."

Five steps more and there stood seven elk, looking right at us. Chriss threw up his gun, first on one and then the another, one after another, all seven of them. I said, "Shoot the first one NOW!" I nudged him in the butt with my foot. Bang went his gun and down went his elk.

Chriss took off like a bird for that elk. I jumped and grabbed his coattail and jerked him to a stop. "Stand and keep your

sight on that elk till you're sure he's down for good," I told him.
When I was satisfied the elk wouldn't get up, I showed Chriss how to get a tree between him and the elk's head so he could sneak up close, always keeping himself covered and out of sight until he was close enough to finish the job with a shot in the back of the head. Chriss did a fine job of this and now can brag about some mighty fine eating meat.

We stood there admiring the elk and I patted him on the back for doing a good job and I started thinking that he was sure accepting the accolades with the grace of a hunter. But finally, I said, "What are you standing here for? Aren't you going to dress him out?"

"I don't know how," he came back, dragging out his knife.

"I'll tell you Chriss, it's nice and warm now. Give me your knife and we'll take our time and I'll show you how to do it right and you'll have no trouble next year."

I took it step by step and he sure paid attention.

When I cut over the brisket and down the neck I said, "Chriss, hold this front foot out of my way. Take your other hand and pull the skin back so I won't cut off a bunch of short hair while I'm taking out his windpipe."

All of a sudden that front foot was flopping around and hitting me in the face. I looked up at Chriss and he was as white as a sheet and shivering; his teeth were even chattering.

"What's the matter Chriss, are you cold?"

"No, no. I just can't s-stop s-s-shaking. I d-d-don't know w-w-what's the matter with me."

You talk about buck fever. He sure had it! I was laughing, but I thought, "That's alright Chriss. We've all experienced it or we would never hunt."

I showed him how to lay the carcass on its back and cover it so the birds couldn't eat any of it and also how to keep the rain and snow out of the body cavity.

While I was cleaning the knife and my hands, in the snow, I said, "Ain't you going to tag it?"

He said, "Yes," and started to tie the tag on a leg.

I rubbed blood over his face and said, "Now you're a hunter."

What are we going to do now?" Chriss asked.

"We're going after your dad and Al 'cause he made me promise I wouldn't load an elk by myself," I said. "We've had the fun, we'll let him do the work."

He laughed and I could see that he sure wanted to tell someone about his elk.

While driving down the road, I said, "Chriss, now when John asks you what you shot, you tell him a five-point bull elk."

" But it's just a bull calf," Chriss said.

I said, "No, it's got a point on each foot and one point on its nose. Now that's five points ain't it?"

"You're right!" Chriss said.

When we drove up in the log yard and John saw all the blood and a big smile on Chriss' face, he dropped his power saw and he and Chriss rolled around, wrestling on the ground. John pounded him on the back.

"What did you get?" John asked.

Chriss responded, "A five-point bull!"

"Oh, no, you didn't."

"Oh yes, I did!"

And away we went again, John as happy as the kid.

When we got back to the woods, I picked a road around stumps, over logs and back up to where we'd left the elk. John hopped out and jerked the fir boughs off the elk and hollered at Chriss, "This ain't no five-point bull!"

Chriss explained, "He's a bull ain't he?" He showed his father how to count the points. Another wrestling match ensued, but we finally got the elk to John's and the shop. Out of the house came Chriss' mom and little sisters to look at the elk. Finally, little Ruth says to Chriss, "How'd you get blood all over your face?"

Chriss told her and she took one look at me and headed for the house, with the other sister following. And I know that I'll still have a hunting partner for years ahead. I watched the girls go into the house and, as I started to count — if I hunt with them all — I figured there's about 14 years ahead of me.

And I thought of the fun I'd just had. And will have!

THE SAGA OF BROWNIE

One day at a horse sale in Missoula I'd bought some saddle horses and, thinking we had enough, I was shooting the bull with some other guys in the corner of the sale ring. Howard Raiser, the auctioneer, hollered over the speaking system, "Copenhaver, here's one for you. Look at that rein on this horse, sure has a handle on him."

I look around and saw this old guy showing the brown horse — a horse that would stop any cowboy and make him look. The horse had a body, fret, legs and neck you couldn't find a fault in. Also, he had a very intelligent head set, just right on his long arched neck. He carried his head like royalty. There was a lot of hot blood in those veins and it sure showed.

I mouthed him and his teeth said he was six, going on seven years of age. Prime age, good physical condition. Just what we needed. When he rode him through the sale ring, did he have a handle on him! Very few horses I've ever seen would rein as smooth as this old pony. Left, then right, spin on his hind quarters, legs well tucked under his body and it seemed he didn't even need those two front feet that worked so smoothly together.

I said to my son, Steve, "There's got to be something wrong with this nag or the guy wouldn't sell him. I bid him in at $475.00, got him, and was pleased with my deal. He was some horse.

Well, we loaded him and the others in the truck and headed up the river for home. When we got to our pasture we had to go up the road about a half mile to find a bank to unload on.

Steve said, "You go down and open the gate and I'll ride this brown horse bareback and run the others down the road. He had no bridle, so he just jumped on him with a halter and headed the horses down the road.

I opened the gate and when the new nags saw our old bunch of horses they took off to meet them, bucking and kicking up as fast as they could go. The others came to meet them to say a horse hello.

When Steve got to the gate, the brown horse was prancing and whinnying, wanting to run after his pals. Steve got the halter off and away wents Brownie, picking up and running to catch up to his buddies.

Now, there was a big clump of willows about 30 feet wide and 30 high out in the middle of the meadow. Poor old Brownie was going full steam ahead and he hit that willow bush head-on right in the middle, flopped over backwards, staggered to his feet

Horses and frisky young colts, corrals and the moutains have been a standard part of Howard's lifestyle in what he calls Copenhaver Country.

and finally trotted over to the rest of his friends. We laughed as it really was a funny sight with all of the horses and mules getting acquainted. We shut the gate and went home.

About a week or so later I got a call from one of my brothers. He said, "You know that brown horse you put in the pasture? He's out in the middle of the meadow right where you left him and he hasn't moved. I don't think he's even been to the creek to get a drink."

I picked up Steve and we went up to have a look. Sure enough, Brownie was standing right where he stopped after his tussle with the willow bush.

We put a rope around his neck and led him over to the creek for a drink. When he'd put his nose down and touch the running water, he'd jerk his head back. He acted like it scared him. We led him out into the tall grass again and when he went to graze, as soon as a blade of grass hit his nose he'd jerk his head up and wouldn't eat. We sure were baffled as to what was wrong.

I said, "I think he's blind."

Steve said, "His eyes are good. Just as clear as any horse."

Well, we took him to the vet. I asked, "Is this horse blind?"

After looking his eyes over, the doc said, "His eyes are good but I think he is stone blind."

You couldn't make him bat his eyes or move his head when you waved your hand at his eyes.

Finally the doc says, "I don't know what's the matter but he's sure enough blind. You might as well can him."

Now, he was too poor to sell so we took him home. If you watered him in a bucket and fed him hay and grain in a manger, he ate and drank fine. We put a few pounds on him and in a month or two took him to a sale. I had to tell them he was blind but they ran him through as a canner. I got the full sum of $10.00 for him — a real deal if you subtract $475.00 plus trucking and feed from that $10.00. It didn't stack up so good at the bank.

This was all a big puzzle, so I kept watching for the guy that had run him through the ring in the first place. One day at a

L. Drake-Robinson © 96

sale I spotted him. I cornered him and said, "I'm the guy that bought that blind horse from you. He was a great animal as you know. I got took, but I'm not sore. I would just like to know what the story is on him. What was wrong with his eyes?"

He laughed and said, "It's a long story but here it is."

I said, "I got lots of time. This is why I'm here."

"Well, I owned this saddle mare that had produced some top saddle stock so I bred her to a big thoroughbred stud and when the time came for her to foal, I was gone for a couple of days. When I returned, the wife and kids were nursing the scrawny colt. They wrapped him up in a blanket to keep him warm and were milking the mare and bottle feeding him. I told them we'd have to put him down. He'd never live. But I could see right then it would be a divorce and the loss of two kids if I did that, so I said to myself, 'Let them fool with him. He'll die anyway.'

"Well, he didn't. In a week he was up nursing. He was spry and frolicking around the stall. I paid no more attention to him but the kids were playing with him and by the time he was six months old, the smallest one was riding him. He'd follow them like a dog. They'd just lay their hand on his neck and guide him where ever they wanted.

"He acted sort of funny when he'd become separated from the old mare or the kids. He'd just stand in the same place till one of them showed up. I examined him and found out he was blind as a bat, born that way. By now there was no way I could dispose of him. He was part of the family.

"When he was past two I decided to try and break him to ride. Well, he responded so well he became my top corral horse when I worked cattle in the corral. Never tried to ride him outside. Always fed him in the barn and watered him in the trough. He fully depended upon me for everything he did. Guess I was his eyes. If I headed him straight at a barn wall he'd hit it head on. He trusted me for everything. If he'd had eyes, you couldn't have bought him for love nor money. The vets all told me there was no connection between his eyes and brain — kind of like a flashlight without any batteries."

PUMPKIN PATCH

Several years ago I got a phone call from a fellow in Spokane, Washington. It seemed they were having a meeting of the North Idaho Outfitters, U.S. Forest Service and U.S.Fish and Wildlife people in Coeur d'Alene, Idaho, and wanted me to give a talk on how an outfitter gets along with bear in grizzly country. Now I've spent my life in grizzly country in the Bob Marshall and Scapegoat Wilderness areas, even before those places were ever thought of as anything except the South Fork Country. They offered to give me expense money and a hotel room for overnight. I agreed and told Marg, "Let's get out of all this snow and ice. The house needs airing out anyway."

So we left early in the morning. I was supposed to meet them at the Pumpkin Patch in Coeur d'Alene at 2 p.m. in the afternoon. We got there about 1:30 and when we walked in, a gentleman met us and said to me, "Would you mind if instead of a speech we put you on a panel of five authorities and have the audience ask questions?"

I said, "I don't care. I'm already here, so do it as you choose."

About 2:30 we took our places at the table in the front of the room. We had a large crowd of sportsmen and outfitters before us. I said to myself, "I wonder what's going to happen?" We were introduced to each other and the crowd.

On my right was a young lady who was head mogul over grizzly bear preservation and the reintroduction of wolves covering Idaho and Montana west of the Continental Divide to the Canadian border. On my left was a forest ranger from Spokane. Next to him was the man next under this lady for grizzly and wolves. On his left was a young fellow who was manager for grizzly bear in Glacier National Park. He also had the job of tracking down the lone wolf that had been reported ranging somewhere in the Selway-Bitterroot Area of central Idaho.

Now, I almost forgot to tell you at first that this event took place about the time hunting grizzly in Montana was stopped and a great push was building to transplant wolves from Canada — literally reintroducing them to Montana and northern Idaho. Now here I was, an old outfitter in the middle of a bunch of pros.

Well, the questions started coming, mostly directed at the lady on my right. Suddenly I realized her answers were completely wrong and that she knew nothing about bear of any kind, and regarding wolves, it was obvious she had only dreams.

I turned to her when she answered a question and said,

Howard's experience with the wilderness and wildlife, such as grizzly bears, comes from firsthand experience. Here's a scene of the Chinese Wall in the Bob Marshall Wilderness, one of his favorite haunts.

"Lady, you are mistaken. That is not so."

I saw the red coming up her neck and she said, "It is too, I've studied these bears."

I thought, silently, "Uh oh," and asked her, out loud, "Lady, have you ever seen a grizzly?"

She sort of stammered and said, "Well, not really."

I asked, "Have you ever seen a black bear or wolf?"

She said, "Well, not really, but I was in Yellowstone Park for two weeks."

I asked, "Didn't you see any bear or bear tracks?"

She says, "No, I was writing my thesis and didn't get around much."

I asked, "How come, if you've never seen even a bear track or a wolf, are you the Number One administrator of both when you don't even know what you're administrating?"

She said, "Oh, we've lots of material we can study."

My answer: "Did you ever realize that the guy that wrote that material might not know any more about it than you?"

The crowd really came down on her hard. I really felt sorry for her and somewhat ashamed for my part in it. But, after the meeting I cornered her and we had a nice visit. She was a very intelligent and smart gal who had degrees and the political pull to get a good job.

Now I wonder about these guys running for president — if they know just the same. As I sit here listening to these jokers tell the American public who should be our next president, and also what dirty rats their opponents are and what they've done wrong, and then "Why I'm the right guy" — I think that I've got the right to blow my horn, too.

Does the phrase "Endangered Species" ring a bell with you? It sure does with me, loud and clear. I figure myself an environmentalist and wilderness advocate, but not as I interpret these phrases today. I've spent over three-quarters of a century in the wilderness and with all our game animals. When they told me wolves were extinct in the Lower 48 states, I knew better. I know they were here when I was born and are still here. Forget the

This aerial view of prime grizzly country in the Bob Marshall Wilderness is the sort of terrain in which Howard has spent countless hours over the years.

transplants. I believe in full protection for the grizzly bear and other animals, but not to the extent of over-running the country and people.

These two topics bring out fire and brimstone at many meetings in Montana, but also some with much humor and the exposure of poor management. While at a meeting of this nature in Great Falls, Montana, a lady was really giving her all-out to protect the grizzly along the eastern front of the Rockies. This one rancher was really giving her a hard time. Apparently, he was a rancher in that area and had lost some cattle due to the grizzly and he sure didn't love them bear at all.

He stood leaning against the wall, wearing an old sunburnt brown hat and run-over cowboy boots. You know he'd been there just by his dress. He'd completely lost his temper with what the lady was saying and he said, "The only good bear is a damn dead one." She came back, "Why Mr. Rogers, where would we be if there were no grizzly?" He tips his hat back on his head and answers, "Why, lady, I guess we'd be up to our ass in huckleberries." You should have heard that crowd. You'd have thought Will Rogers had just come on stage.

At another meeting there was a rancher who was seeking help from the crowd because of transplanted wolves. It seems that he fed his cattle hay on a meadow about two miles from his house. Now this feed ground was packed down to solid frozen ice and snow, just like cement. If you've ever seen a feed ground in March you'll know what I'm talking about. Well, this one morning when he went to feed the cows their hay, he found a dead cow with two wolves feeding on it. Both wolves had collars on them, meaning they were transplants. He dashed back to the house and called the game warden, who said, "I'll be right out."

Two days later, here came Mr. Game Warden and a lad from the U.S. Fish and Wildlife Service wanting to look at the cow. By this time, the magpies and eagles were feeding on the carcass. He showed them where what remained of the cow was and went on with his work. A couple hours later, the two officials showed up again. The rancher asked, "What did you find?" This lad from the U.S. Fish and Wildlife Service says, "I'm sorry to tell you but we've found that the magpies killed your cow."

Whether he was ever paid for his cow I do not know. One thing I do know. This old boy didn't think we needed any more wolves in Montana.

Mebby you better go get your salt shaker for this next one. It happened right close to where I live and was told to me by a guy who said he was there. We have always been blessed by lots of mountain lions in this country, but since they deemed them a game animal and put a quota on them we've got them everywhere, even in town. Well, this trapper friend of mine caught a yearling cat in his coyote trap. Having no lion license, he called the game warden and told the warden where it was and asked him to turn it loose. Well, the game warden took a live bear trap and pickup and went after Mr. Lion. He finally got the cat out of the trap and stuffed into the bear cage and went home and parked the rig in front of the garage until the next morning, when the big boss told him to just turn the cat loose again.

Not thinking too good, he went out and opened the door on the trap. Out leapt Mr. Lion just as a rancher drove up in his pickup with his Blue Heeler dog in the back end. As the cat cleared the cage, that dog took him and around the truck went the cat, with the dog in hot pursuit. The garage door was open and in went Mr. Cat and he quickly leapt up to the rafters. They called off the dog but couldn't get the cat out of the garage.

The game warden went into the house and called Missoula for help. Somebody there told him to sit tight as a guy would be sent out with a tranquilizer gun. Meanwhile, being that it was now so nice and peaceful, Mr. Cat sneaked out and started for the woods, but Fido was still awake and after that pussy he scrambled. Mr. Puss Cat saw the open door to the house and in he went, with Fido right behind him. The cat made a turn or two around the downstairs but, liking higher ground, upstairs he scrambled with the dog close behind. Things were a bit mixed up then and when they got there with the tranquilizer gun, it wouldn't work.

Mr. Rancher went over to the pickup and hauled out his

.357 and upstairs he went. This gun worked. The windows rattled with the explosion and you could hear a bumpety-bump as down the stairs came Mr. Cat, being drug by the tail. The rancher dragged him up to the game warden and said, "Here's your damn cat. Go plant him where you please."

Now I know that some people are going to say this is a sorehead writing. I'll be honest with you. I sure don't go along with some of these wilderness and environmental ideas we have today. May I present a couple of reasons for you to think about?

The South Fork of the Flathead River and White River are worldly known for the terrific cutthroat and Dolly Varden fishing. I've fished both for 75 years and have eaten many a fish. Before me, many another person had done the same. It was the great fishing area for the Flathead and Blackfoot Indians for how many years I don't know.

I well remember, when I was young, the Flathead Indians fishing the South Fork and White River, drying and smoking the fish they packed out for winter food. I knew some of those "Old Longhairs," as they were called, very well — some wonderful woodsmen and gentlemen.

About 17 or 18 years ago the newspapers and radio were warning people not to eat any fish caught in the White River or the lower South Fork because some "bugoligist" had tested the White River and determined it was contaminated with mercury. There are no roads, no mining, no timber harvest in any of those drainages. Why the mercury? It has always been there!

More recently, television and the news media proclaimed the Blackfoot River running past my home was the worst contaminated river in the Northwest. High in mercury. Well, another analysis was made of the headwaters right up where Landers Fork runs out of Olson Peak in the Scapegoat Wilderness Area and the water tested more mercury content than it did at the confluence of the Bitterroot and Clark Fork rivers.

Up there on Olson Peak there are no mines, no roads, no timber harvest. Why the high mineral content? Montana is loaded with minerals. Minerals have always been in the water and always will be.

OVANDO MOUNTAIN

I just got back from the "Ovando Senior Citizens Center," which is more commonly known as "Trixi's Antler Saloon." We don't have a regular senior center in Ovando, but "Trixi's" sure fills the bill. One can pick up a lot of senior gossip there — like, who died, who didn't, whose wife ran off with whose husband, and who shot an elk in hunting season, or out of season, for that matter.

Trixi's is usually open by 10 o'clock in the winter and there is always some old-timers dropping in shortly after.

Now this morning I was a little early and expected to be the first one there. But when I drove up, there was no place to park except out in the middle of the yard. I could hear people laughing and carrying on inside when I stepped out of my car. I wondered if those people had stayed there all night, or if there was an old-fashioned wake going on, or just what? Then I noticed some foreign license plates on a pickup in the parking lot, and said, "I know that rig." Sure enough, when I opened the door and stepped in, I was greeted by a number of voices, all at the same time, saying, "Hello Howard."

There, sitting on the stools, were Shorty, Julio, Shirley, Dar (Shorty's wife) and some others, laughing and having a good time while Leo and the girls are getting breakfast set out for them.

Shorty and Julio are brothers from Minnesota, who, for how many years I don't recall, have come out to Montana each season on a hunting trip. They set up a big camp up the other side of Ovando Mountain. They've always got some saddle mules and hunt for elk and deer on both Ovando Mountain and Elk

Mountain. Their friends from back home visit them at the camp and hunt a few days, and then someone else shows up. It's never been a very dull camp and every time I've stopped by they sure seem to have been busy because the dishes are always dirty and on the table.

I said, "What are you doing out here in the middle of winter?"

Shorty said, "Gettin' married."

"Couldn't you find a warmer place to get married than here? If'n you wanted to get married in the snow you had it at home. By the news you've got more snow than we have," I said.

"We wanted to get married out here," Shorty said.

Hold it! I really started to write this about Shirley and her hunt last fall. I'll pick up the wedding later.

Now Shirley is not a big gal, about 16 inches short of 6'2", sort of feisty, a little redhead that loves to hunt deer. She'd never shot an elk but this year she applied for a cow permit and lucked out. Now she was all set to go get her first elk.

She drove up above Shorty's camp on an old logging road, parked the rig and took off. She hadn't gone far in the snow, which was about five inches deep, when she came upon these big deer tracks. They sure look fresh, she said to herself, "Hold it! I'm hunting elk. Those are elk tracks and I've got a cow tag. Sure hope it's a cow."

Everybody had told Shirley to go slow when hunting elk, take one step at a time and look every place for that tell-tale orange rump. She went over this little ridge, down through a dense thicket, and then up over another hill. When just about to the top of the hill, she sees an old logging road. "I'll sit me down and take a rest when I get to that road," Shirley thought. At last, she got to the top of the hill and looked for a place to sit.

"Whoa! What's that?" she whispered to herself. What she was looking at moved. It was that big orange rump they'd been telling her about — an elk. Up came Shirley's gun and she lined up her sight on that yellowish side but she couldn't shoot. She was looking uphill and there was a big log between her and the elk, with about six inches of snow covering her target. What should she do? If she moved, the cow will see her as it was looking her way. "Oh, hell. I'll shoot right through that log," Shirley thought and, Ker-Boom, she touched the rifle off.

When the snow settled, the elk was gone and Shirley was afraid to go look for fear she only wounded it. She was standing there trying to work up courage to go after the elk when, down the hill below her she sees an old black hat bobbing along. She hollers, "Help, help," and up the hill came this guy Shorty.

"I think I shot an elk," explained Shirley.

"Why don't you go look?" Shorty asked.

"I don't know what to do if it's just wounded or how to dress it, if I got it," she said.

"I'll help you. Where was it?"

She showed him the log and when he inspected it, she'd shot right through the snow, missing the log. When he went a bit farther, there were elk tracks in the snow. The elk was headed out of there, fast, but there was blood, on either side of the tracks, in the snow. Mebby five or six jumps down the hill lay Shirley's big, fat cow. And now the fun began.

She conned Shorty into dressing it for her. Shorty said, "Now, you get right close and watch everything I do cause I don't want nobody sayin' I showed you wrong."

Shirley is right behind him sort of squatted down in the snow. He cut off a big piece of the bloody guts and threw it over his shoulder, hitting her on the face and head, blood all over. She jumped up and this lying Shorty apologized as best he could without laughing.

Now, Shirley is an accomplished hunter. I asked her this morning, "How was your elk meat?"

She sort of made a face and says, "I like deer meat the best. Elk is more wild. I've given most of it away to my friends."

"Did they like it?"

She says, "I think so but really don't know, but it sure makes me feel good when they brag about what a good hunter I am. Sort of boosts my ego."

Back to Shorty.

Seems they planned to get married riding two mules up on Ovando Mountain. Can you imagine people who want to get married in two and a half feet of snow on a 7,000 foot mountain when it's 10 or 12 degrees below zero, Fahrenheit? My friend, a marriage like this sure ought to last. Congratulations to you both and the wedding party. Me, I'd have found a nice warm hotel and let the formalities wait for summertime.

Now behind this pickup is an enclosed horse trailer. I said, "Shorty, why the horse trailer? It's empty. Didn't you have time to unhook it when you left?"

He said, "Oh, we'll fill it up before we get home."

I'll tell you something. I think Julio should have taken this boy out behind the barn and told him a thing or two about life, cause if he thinks his family is going to increase that much before he gets home, he's got another think coming.

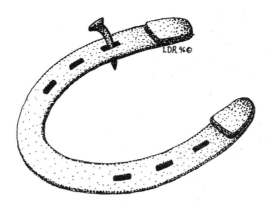

SHOEING HORSES

When we were kids, we had two saddle horses that we rode everywhere. Now when I say we rode them, I really mean "rode." We did not use them just to warm our butts on a frosty morning. Gene wasn't so hard on them as Lawrence and I were. We didn't have time to go at a walk anyplace; it was wide open, as hard as they could run. But both those horses, St. Elmo and Comet, were carrying a lot of hot blood in their veins and loved to run.

Anytime we came upon someone mounted, he was challenged for a race right on the spot.

St. Elmo usually won but it was few times that Comet even looked at the tail-end of any other horse. They both loved to run and were sure in running shape at all times.

We milked a bunch of cows for the cream and fed the horses milk and grain most every day. I'll tell you, if you can get a horse to drink milk its coat of hair will shine and be slick and smooth.

In the summer time they'd get footsore, so Pop would have to tack on some shoes. Finally he said, "You boys come with me," and out to the barn we went. He got his shoeing gear and showed us how to trim and shoe old Comet. Then he said, "If you're big enough to ride these horses you're big enough to shoe them. St. Elmo needs shoes, so get at it."

Well, Gene and I finally got him shod, sort of a rough looking job but he had iron on his feet anyway. But it didn't take too many of these sessions to learn how to do the job; we were slow but could do as good as the next guy.

One day I was out there tacking on some shoes when our

grandparents came driving in from Great Falls. So Grandad came out to see how I was doing. As I remember, I was using a regular claw hammer to drive the nails. He looked at the job and went over to his car. When he came back, he said, "Here, you can have this shoeing hammer." He showed me a few tricks of the trade to make it easier and better. When I was done he told me this story:

"Many years ago when I was an 18-year-old boy and leaving home to come to America from Wales, my father handed me a leather apron wrapped around this hammer, a rasp and a pair of hoof nippers and said, 'Son, keep these always. You can always make a living anyplace in the world because every country has horses and all horses need shoes.' I have worn out many a rasp and nipper but I want you to have this hammer and keep it."

I still have that old hammer today, and still use it — several

This scene from the Copenhaver Ranch in 1947 shows not only the awesome setting of their operation in the Ovando area, but indicates the significance of keeping their large remuda of horses shod.

new handles later, of course, but the head shines from use and care. I've shod many horses and mules each spring, summer and fall, every year of my life — how many thousand I do not have the foggiest of an idea. But this I do know: something that is good will last forever if taken care of. Grandad left Wales at 18, which would make this old hammer around 150 years old.

In the heyday of my outfitting business I had 120 to 130 mules and horses that needed shoeing three times a year and sometimes four, depending on how many trips we had booked. Most of them were good to shoe but I had a few that were real stinkers. We'd shoe all the good ones first and when we got to the tough boys, two of us would work together.

Now, one time Ted and I were shoeing this big 16-hand, 1,400-pound mule and he was a fighter with a capital F. We had a front foot tied up and I was nailing on the shoe. Ted was off to the side, holding the foot rope light. Well, just as I hit a nail with the hammer, Jack, the mule, gave a big jump and up in the air he went, about five feet high. Old Ted sat down on that rope right at the top of his jump.

This turned the mule flat on his side, way up in the air. Down came old Jack. He landed flat on his side and it sounded like he broke every bone in his body. His legs stuck out stiff and straight. He sort of quivered all over and then slowly relaxed and his eyes rolled back up in his head. Then the stiffness went out of his legs and they fell limp. Ted put his hand on the mule's nostril. I felt for pulse in his throat. None. I said, "Dead as a doornail."

Ted said, "Shall I pull those shoes? We can use them on another mule. They're brand new."

I said, "Might as well pull them."

As Ted started to pull the first shoe, old Jack came alive and was on his feet like a flash, snorting and blowing and kicking at Ted. Ted said, as he ducked out of Jack's way, "If'n you want them new slippers you can have them."

Another time we had this big dapple grey horse, a beautiful pile of horse flesh as I'd ever seen but you changed your mind once you tried to shoe him. You could tie one hind foot right up to his neck, then stand up next to his head on the other side, hold a hammer in your hand and point it back toward his shoulder and that old pony would stand on his front feet and kick that hammer out of your hand so quick one couldn't believe it.

We would four-foot him and lay him on the ground, tie all four feet together and run a pole between his legs. Then we'd tie one end of the pole to the top of a corral post. With him laying on his back, all four feet in the air, we'd trim his feet and tack on the shoes. When we let him up he'd just shake, heave a big sigh and be just as nice to handle as could be. He just didn't want anyone playing with his toes.

Then there was Gene's saddle mare. She was a sweetheart, easy riding, handled smooth as silk and lots of fire. But when it came to getting a pair of shoes she was a wildcat. Mean, fast and treacherous. Kick, strike and bite. We tried everything on her. Finally, we noticed if she was sore-footed she didn't fight so much or hard.

So one day when we were going to have to shoe her Gene said, "I'm going to ride her to Ovando and make her good and foot sore. So down the road he went. He ran her down the gravel road and back. When he returned she was foot sore alright. Her feet were almost smoking — real hot, but that old heifer stood good while we put new plates on all four feet. From then on, you know she had sore feet before every shoeing for sure.

We had another good mule called Patches — a big pinto mule (see her story elsewhere in the book). When you shod her, it took about an acre of ground and lots of rope to tie those feet up and she'd fight till that last nail was clinched.

When winter came and the snow started to build up on the steel shoes, you'd pull all the shoes off all the stock and let them go barefoot all winter. Usually when it came time to do this, you'd have the stock in the corral and just catch the first animal handy and start pulling shoes.

Now old Patches would see what was going on and come over to where you were working, and rub you with her head. I'd chase her off and she'd come right back. Well, I'd pick up a front foot and pull the shoe. You didn't even need to put a halter on her. She'd stand till you pulled the last one, then snort and blow, wheel away from you and kick at you — never hitting you. She just let you know who was in charge.

The Table
Well, I got tired of all this back-breaking work shoeing, putting on bandaids, and having so many bruised spots on me that a neighbor and I developed a shoeing table. This table was just like a cattle chute, only you tied the horse to one side of the chute with two big wide belts around its body, with its head tied to the

At work putting shoes on a rough one on the Copenhaver Ranch.

table — which is one side of the chute. Then, you open the gate and a motor turns the table down flat, horse and all. While the table is being laid over, one fellow ties the horse's front feet solid to it. After the table is laid over, you strap the hind feet down. Now the horse can do nothing but struggle a little. All four feet are sticking out where you can trim and shoe them.

If you want, four men can shoe at the same time. We use an electric sander to level the feet and with two of us working, you have the horse immobilized for anywhere from nine to twelve minutes. Speed is what counts because if you take too long the horse or mule will get tired and start to fight the table, causing you some trouble. We generally shoe about 30 head a day using the table.

The nice thing about this way of shoeing is that, if a horse needs corrective shoeing, it usually is nasty to shoe. With the table you can take your time and do a good job and the horse can't hurt you or itself because the table is padded with four inches of foam rubber under a felt topping.

For the last 20 or so years, I have shod commercially wherever they have big bunches of stock — usually from 50 to 250 head. Dude ranches, outfitters and Yellowstone Park have been our biggest clients.

You never know what you are going to experience in stock or help. One year we pulled into Roosevelt Lodge in Yellowstone Park where we had 250-some head to do. It was a wet, rainy season and the corrals were eight inches deep in mud. They feed hay all the time so the only time the horses are out of that mud is when people are riding them.

Now the mud collects in the hair above their hooves and they get an infection that is contagious, and all the horses become lame.

Well the boss man asked me and Dan, "What am I going to do? I need these horses."

I said, "If they were mine I'd have some of these guys you got standing around here put them in that stock tank and wash their legs and feet with a garden hose. Then I'd clip all the hair off their fetlocks and, with disinfectant, I'd treat them all and you'll clear up the sore ankles."

He agreed that my suggestion was a great idea. Well, me and Dan are shoeing when all of a sudden I noticed a commotion across the way. I said, "Dan, look at that."

There were five of those eastern cowgirls the Park Service had hired as wranglers. Each had a little animal clipper working on this one old pony in that chute. Some of them were sitting on the ground under Dobbin, shaving all four legs at once.

That old pony's eyes were bugged out of his head like a frog's — scared to death. Well, now these cow-ladies went through that whole bunch of nags, never once got kicked, stepped on or anything. And these are range horses, not someone's docile pet. Some of those old canners sure would have killed you or me if we'd tried it. Guess God just takes care of kids and damn fools.

These gals were sitting underneath these old ponies, laughing and giggling, talking up a storm — never realizing what could have happened.

The boss came by, shaking his head, and said, "I'll believe anything from now on."

I got a call one day from a friend of mine who was a rodeo producer. Seems he'd bought 22 wild stallions from the Bureau of Land Management down in Idaho. The deal was, you had to keep them for a year before you could sell them. Well, Claude built this big corral boarded up 14 feet high to hold them in but he soon found out he had to separate them because some of those wild horses were so mean they'd kill each other. After he'd had them a year, he called me and asked if I could castrate them wild buggers.

I said sure, but we'd have to set up a chute of some kind to get them out of the corral and onto the table.

He said, "I've got a two horse bucking chute here. We can rig that up and it will work."

I said, "Fine. When you ready?"

"Right now," he said. He was eager to get the job done.

I told him I'd be there about seven in the morning.

Horses were the main mode of transportation in the back country.

"Okay," he said. "I'll have the chute set up when you get here."

The next morning I was there early and we got everything all set up. Now these old nags ain't never had a halter on them, let alone being broke to lead. We'd run them into the chute out of the corral, then into the chute and onto the shoeing table. I'd stand beside the gate on the table and when they ran into the chute I'd throw a wet blanket over their head. Not being able to see, they would just freeze and stand still — and before they realized anything we had them strapped to the table. By noon we had altered 22 stallions and were having a cool beer at the house when the phone rang.

It was Marg and she told me she's advised an old gal that I would stop that afternoon and shoe her two Arabian horses. Now prior to this I'd told this lady I did not want to shoe her fancy nags. If I'd skin one of them a little bit I'd never hear the last of it.

But I said, "Okay, I'll stop and see her."

Marg said they're in the corral, two to put shoes on and one colt they want trimmed, but that the people involved might not be there when I got to the old gal's place.

Now, I drove up to their house and set up my table. No one was there, so I went ahead and shod the two horses. Then I was just about through putting the trim on the colt when up drove this gal and her daughter.

They looked the shod horses over and petted and cooed to them. Then they came over to the table where I was letting the colt off to the ground. I led him over and tied him to the fence and, as I went back to the table, I noticed these two gals with their heads close together, talking.

Now remember, I'd just come from altering 22 stud horses and there was plenty of blood on that table.

The lady asked, "Where did all the blood come from?"

I said, nonchalantly, "Oh, I had a little tough luck this morning and killed a couple of horses."

She paid me on the spot but never called to have me shoe

those horses of hers again. Guess she must have believed me. Funny too, because so many people don't.

LIFE IS EASY

This old trail I've led has sure been an easy one, except when I was a slick-eared kid with the desire to become a top bronc rider and cowboy. Now there was nothing to achieving those goals, I told myself time and again, except for someone to practice and use their brains, if they had enough. But, it seemed to me that I had been asleep under the table when they dished out the plate of brains.

So, I took a job breaking a string of horses to ride for a rancher close by. For real money, too. I'd ride them all for thirty days for $10.00 a head. You add that up and it came to $60.00, but then think of the experience I got.

All went well on the job until I got to a little bay pony I called Shorty. He was something else. It seemed, to me, that he had been around and that he got the brains I'd missed.

He tried everything in the book — kick, bite, buck and bawl. But I finally got the buck ridden out of him and thought I had it made. Then he started to stampede with me; he'd take his head and you couldn't turn him or stop him till he ran down. It was kind of like driving a car with no brakes or steering wheel.

One day we were going out across this big flat pasture land just full of big rocks when old Shorty took his head and away we went. He was running blind and those rocks were flying up by me! I sat back on those reins and the bit parted right in the middle of his mouth, so I grabbed him by the brow band and his ears. But he was really getting it into high gear, so I stood up in my stirrups, rocked my weight from side to side then threw my weight to the right side, throwing him flat on his side on the ground.

The installation early in life of basic family and eduational values came to Howard as a natural part of growing up in a rural setting like Ovando. In this photo of the Copenhaver family, from left in the back row are Gene, Lawrence and Howard, their mother, and the unnamed teacher. In the foreground at left are Wendell and Louise.

I hung on to the saddle and neck rope and came out on top. And when he struggled to his feet, I had a loop on his nose and good footing. It took about a week before I could walk straight up and had grown skin back on my arms and legs, but at the moment I savored my victory. That episode had sure put the big cure on Shorty.

Another time, I was shoeing horses and reached down for a belt. This was a nice gentle horse, but I didn't move fast enough and that son-of-a-buck kicked me and broke my arm right above the wrist.

A guy drove me to the doctor's office and when I walked up to the desk, the receptionist said, "Can I help you?"

I said, "Yes, I want to see a doctor. I broke my arm. (I was holding my wrist so it wouldn't fall down.)

While the author writes that "Life Is Easy," there has been plenty of work involved, too. Here's a family photo from earlier days that shows the Copenhavers cutting wood for the winter. From left are Gene and Lawrence Copenhaver, Frank Boisrence, Wendell Copenhaver, Howard's father holding Leon, and Harold Haynes sitting on the log.

She said, "How do you know it's broken?"

I just let go of it and it flopped down like a door hinge. Her mouth flew open and she said, "Have a seat. I'll get a doctor."

Along came another gal, who led me to a room and said, "The doctor will be right here." And off she went.

Right back she came with a stack of papers and a pen, and asked me to fill out those sheets of paper before the doctor came in. Again, I let my arm drop and said, "Lady, I can't write left-handed. Now get that doctor!"

She flew out of there and came right back with the doctor. She said, "I'm sorry. I never thought."

On another occasion, we got out of the hills late in the evening with a large party of guests and by the time we were loading the stock to haul them home from the trailhead, it was dark. Now I mean dark, just as black as the insides of a cow. We were loading this horse trailer and had a young mule that had never been loaded before. I was trying to lift his front foot up on the trailer floor, hoping that he wouldn't kick when the two kids sicked the dog on him. But when they did, that blue heeler hit his hind leg and I guess you know who was kicked underneath him.

The dog wouldn't stop and I never knew a mule had so many feet. Every time I ducked one, I got another one from someplace else. One of the men grabbed my leg and drug me out of that pile of feet. If I hadn't been hurting so bad, at the time I'd have killed two kids and a dog.

This kind of treatment has gone on and on, and any old outfitter can tell you the same. Now, the years have rolled by and I have mellowed. I quit working these rough horses and I don't even like to fight with my wife; I've got some grandkids now and life has sort of smoothed out.

Last winter, a year ago, I got a call from one of the grandkids who was away in college, in Virginia. "Grampa, I have some friends from Sweden who want to come to Montana on vacation next May. Would you take us for a day's ride up to North Fork Falls?"

I said, "Sure, honey. I'll get some saddle horses from Steve (my son) and we'll have a good day."

Well, Steve set me up with six saddle horses and gave me his horse to use myself. He said, "Don't drag your trailer cinch up tight till you've ridden him a couple of miles 'cause he goes along wanting to kick up if it's tight. I said, "Okay," and we climbed on board and up the trail we went. I put Chriss in front as he knew the trail, and I brought up the rear end of the gang.

Now this horse, Dudley, stands 17 hands and weighs in at 1,400 pounds. He's gentle as a kitten, but he's a big quarterhorse with lots of fire and just like a big cat on his feet. We were riding along, enjoying the scenery, when the trail led down a long hill. Just as we broke over the top, Mr. Dudley let out a squeal and

Even in the summer of 1996 the setting of a new Douglas fir tree in the town square in Ovando attracts a collection of observers, including Howard at the far left.

went high into the air.

I pulled on his reins, knowing I was in for a ride. Well, when he came down on that first jump my right knee hit the rump of the horse in front of me and I was pushed right out of the saddle. What did I do but jamb my heels into his flanks; he let out another squeal and headed for the sky again. I knew by then that I'd lost the race and threw myself in a ball so I'd roll when I hit the ground. I flew through the air, over the two riders in front of me, and landed on my right shoulder about 65 feet down the hill. It wasn't the long fall that hurt, it was that sudden stop on that hard trail.

My guests said I turned two somersaults as I went over their heads. Boy, did it hurt. I think it shook all my connections loose inside. I know it tore that tendon over the shoulder and down my arm.

That was the last day of May in 1995. As I write this, it is the 28th day of May in 1996 and I'm still laying on a vibrating pad and rubbing in plenty of horse liniment — hurting more now than I like, but it'll probably get worse. The chiropractor is counting my money and telling me to come back next Friday.

With all the sunshine in an outfitter's life, I guess there has to be some cloudy skies.

DO I OWE SOMEONE

You, me and every other guy, rich man, poor man, beggar man and the millionaire, all owe someone something along the line. There are none of us who are not debtors. Mebby its not money but it amounts to more than that. It's love, respect and gratitude. Some of us are slow to repay them in full; we try to get by as cheap as we can.

I for one owe so much to this little gal of mine.

People pat me on the back for writing books they enjoy. Let me tell you right now, there would be no books if I had to do it myself. She reads them and gets the sentences where they belong, tells me you don't spell cat with a "K" and then there's those hours on the typewriter that I could not master and, above all, encouragement.

Also, she's so honest she'd say, "You can't write it that way. That's not just right." Why she's so honest she won't even let me tell a little white lie. How she puts up with me I'll never know.

Then I can watch her face (and she's got a pretty one) as she reads these stories and say to myself, "Just as well throw that one in File 13."

She's the same girl that stayed and nursed me when I got banged up at a rodeo while all the other boys and girls went to the big dance that night long ago. Also saw me off on the train when I went to war and cried when I called her from the Navy hospital four years later. The same gal who gave me her hand at a wedding where I felt like a burro in a flock of pretty sheep.

She also made that ride in "A Honeymoon on Horseback."

More than half a century ago, Howard carried this picture of his sweetheart, Margaret, to war when he served in the U.S. Navy on a battleship in the Pacific Theater. In photo below, the couple celebrate their Fiftieth Wedding Anniversary.

And rode into Missoula in a rickety old car when the labor pains were only three minutes apart.

By the way, I had a flat tire that day. I jumped out of the car and threw open the trunk. No jack and a flat spare tire. Flagged down a car and he hauled her to the hospital. Never found out the guy's name. He just saw her into the emergency room and left. Bet he was happy. When I limped that old wreck up to the hospital we had a new daughter and Marg didn't even ask me how I got the tire fixed. Don't think she gave a damn.

She also stuck tight when we couldn't pay the grocery bill or fix that old car. But she always had a meal on the table and a smile on her face.

She wrote letters and made telephone calls to prospective guests and convinced them I was their only choice as an outfitter and guide. Kept the books and proved we were right on income taxes. I never did anything but sign the documents where she had her finger.

You talk about a partner. I've never wondered where Marg was in over half a century.

Oh yes, this Scottish-French lady has a temper. You should have been around the summer after I helped her get rid of the weeds in her garden. Seems that when I sprayed them with Roundup an ill breeze that wasn't supposed to came up and drifted some of the spray over to her carrots and beets. You never saw such carrots. Some looked like an old-time corkscrew. Others were short and fat at the top with five or six carrots going in all directions. Unpleasant is a better word for it.

She has a green thumb and the house if full of plants. I always say if the winter is too hard we can bring the horses in the house and save a month's worth of hay, but the garden didn't work that way.

Then there was the time we were hunting, the last day of the season, and an elk walked up and stood broadside to us. I eased the gun over to her and said, "You shoot and if you miss, give it back to me and I'll get it."

Bang! She shot, and missed. The elk was only 25 yards

away. I let go and away went the elk. I missed too! Do you think she's forgotten that? No, my friend.

When she got out of school till we came home after World War II, she was a private secretary — a real city girl, but she changed. She came home to a wood cookstove, making her own bread, cakes, etc., and cooking for me and my two bachelor brothers and a crew of men. It was hard to jump from a typewriter to a stove and a house with outdoor plumbing and gas lights you had to fill each afternoon. No switches to throw. Make lunches, if you had anything to make them out of, and put up with a bunch of lion hounds.

Worked her heart out fixing supper for 6:30 and then nobody would show up to eat till 10:00 o'clock that night, never saying "Thanks" — just stuffing it down and going out.

We've got two kids now and Marg was the school bus to school 20 miles away. Two trips each day. She was driving a "Hope I Can." That's a car or pickup that's supposed to run good. Sun or storm, you've got to go. She did it.

Me, I was trying to make a living, chasing lions, falling timber or pitching hay to some old cows.

Then came a day when she had to go to Missoula, 75 miles away, and pick up some hunters. I said to Pat McNalley, "You go in with Marg and get my pickup at Garden City Motors. It's fixed. You can haul a couple of them hunters and their duffel."

Well, it was dark when Pat came into the saddle shed where I was packing up packs for the trip to hunting camp the next morning.

"How'd you make it?" I asked.

He said, "You're the only man in the world that's got a wife that can drive down the road at 75 miles an hour and whip two kids who are fighting in the back seat."

That's my Marg.

Then there was that day in the hot summertime when she drove to the trailhead with cool lemonade and cookies for us after a hot day on the trail. We didn't show up. We'd decided to stay another day in the hills.

And all the other times we came out a day or two early and she had to feed a big crew with no notice.

Then there's the times I came out of those hills with a bunged up back. She has always been there with the BenGay or aspirin, worrying like an old hen with a dozen chicks as a hawk flies over.

It's still that way 52 years later. Do I owe anybody anything? You guess, I know.

The only thing is, there are no words that can say "Thanks." I just have to believe she knows and feels it the same way I do.

Thanks, Marg and may God bless us both as he has so many times before.

Love, Howard

ABOUT THE ILLUSTRATIONS

The illustrations for *COPENHAVER COUNTRY* are the work of artist Leslie Drake-Robinson. A native Montanan whose grandparents settled in the state at the turn of the century, Leslie was raised with a rich heritage of family stories and an understanding of the trials of frontier life. She began painting early in life and, at age 14, had one of her watercolors selected to become part of the Permanent Collection at the Kennedy Art Center in Washington, D.C. She studied art at both Northern Arizona University and the University of Montana, from which she graduated, with honors, in 1979. After teaching art for five years at high schools in western Montana, on the Flathead Indian Reservation, and in Florence and Missoula, she started a wholesale business selling her artwork on postcards, note cards and limited edition prints. With the help of her husband, Tom, her cards and prints have been marketed across three states and in three national parks. Leslie Drake-Robinson lives with her husband and son in the small town of Grantsdale, near Hamilton, in Montana's Bitterroot Valley.

LISTING OF BOOKS

Additional copies of **COPENHAVER COUNTRY,** *and many other of Stoneydale Press' books on outdoor recreation, big game hunting, or historical reminisces centered around the Northern Rocky Mountain region, are available at many book stores and sporting goods stores, or direct from Stoneydale Press. If you'd like more information, you can contact us by calling a Toll Free number,* **1-800-735-7006,** *or by writing the address at the bottom of the page. Here's a partial listing of some of the books that are available:*

Cookbooks

Camp Cookbook, *Featuring Recipes for Fixing Both at Home and in Camp, With Field Stories by Dale A. Burk, 216 pages, comb binding*

Cooking for Your Hunter, *By Miriam Jones, 180 pages, comb binding*

Historical Reminisces

They Left Their Tracks, *By Howard Copenhaver, Recollections of Sixty Years as a Wilderness Outfitter, 192 pages, clothbound or softcover editions (One of our all-time most popular books.)*

More Tracks, *By Howard Copenhaver, 78 Years of Mountains, People & Happiness, 180 pages, clothbound or softcover editions.*

Indian Trails & Grizzly Tales, *By Bud Cheff Sr., 212 pages, available in clothbound and softcover editions.*

Mules & Mountains, By Margie E. Hahn, the story of Walt Hahn, Forest Service Packer, 164 pages, clothbound or softcover editions

Hunting Books

High Pressure Elk Hunting, *By Mike Lapinski. The latest book available on hunting elk that have become educated to the presence of more hunters working them, 192 pages, many photographs, hardcover or softcover.*

Bugling for Elk, *By Dwight Schuh, the bible on hunting early-season elk. A recognized classic, 164 pages, softcover edition only.*

The Woodsman And His Hatchet, *By Bud Cheff. Subtitled "Eighty Years on Wilderness Survival," this book gives you practical, common sense advice on survival under emergency conditions in the wilderness. Softcover.*

Coyote Hunting, *By Phil Simonski. Presents basics on hunting coyotes as well as caring for the pelts, 126 pages, many photographs, softcover only.*

Elk Hunting in the Northern Rockies, By Ed Wolff. Uses expertise of five recognized elk hunting experts to show the five basic concepts used to hunt elk. Another of our very popular books, 162 pages, many photographs.

So You Really Want To Be a Guide, *By Dan Cherry.* The latest and single most authoritative source on what it takes to be a guide today. This book is an excellent guideline to a successful guiding career. Softcover edition only.

Field Care Handbook For The Hunter & Fisherman, *By Bill Sager & Duncan Gilchrist,* 168 pages, comb binding, many photographs and illustrations. The most comprehensive field care handbook available.

Hunting Open Country Mule Deer, *By Dwight Schuh.* Simply the best and most detailed book ever done for getting in close to big mule deer. The ultimate mule deer book by a recognized master, 14 chapters, 180 pages.

Montana Hunting Guide, *By Dale A. Burk,* the most comprehensive and fact-filled guidebook available on hunting in Montana, 192 pages, clothbound or softcover editions.

Taking Big Bucks, *By Ed Wolff.* Subtitled "Solving the Whitetail Riddle," this book presents advice from top whitetail experts with an emphasis on hunting western whitetails. 176 pages, 62 photographs.

Radical Elk Hunting Strategies, *By Mike Lapinski.* Takes over where other books on early-season elk hunting leave off to give advice on what the hunter must do to adapt to changing conditions. 162 pages, 70 photographs.

Western Hunting Guide, *By Mike Lapinski,* the most thorough guide on hunting the western states available. A listing of where-to-go in the western states alone makes the book a valuable reference tool, 168 pages, clothbound or softcover editions.

STONEYDALE PRESS PUBLISHING COMPANY
523 Main Street • Box 188
Stevensville, Montana 59870
Phone: 406-777-2729